PRAISE FOR

THE 86 PERCENT

SOLUTION

"This book demonstrates that the dramatic differences of emerging markets create tremendous opportunities. The authors present powerful solutions for unlocking these opportunities. The 86 Percent Solution is a wake-up call for any company, consultant, or educational institution that has not given these markets sufficient attention in the past. And it can serve as a rich guidebook for those who want to understand and grow their businesses in the 86 percent world."

—Rajat Gupta, senior partner worldwide, McKinsey & Company, and chairman of the board of the Indian School of Business, Hyderabad

"The 86 Percent Solution makes it abundantly clear that while emerging markets are the future, the path to this future will not be a smooth highway. Emerging nations advance in the balance between tradition and innovation. The solutions presented in this book are based upon a deep understanding of the complexities of these markets. The authors offer insights not only for companies engaged in these markets, but also for policymakers, NGOs, and worldwide organizations that want to understand the role that business can play in innovation and economic development."

—Chandra Babu Naidu, former chief minister, Andhra Pradesh, India

"[The 86 Percent Solution offers] a unique insight for those who need to understand what will be the key driver of the global economy in the first half of the twenty-first century."

—Niall Fitzgerald, chairman of Reuters and former chairman of Unilever

The 86 Percent Solution

The 86 Percent Solution

How to Succeed in the Biggest Market Opportunity of the Next 50 Years

Vijay Mahajan and Kamini Banga
with Robert Gunther

Ideas. Action. Impact.
**Wharton School
Publishing**

Library of Congress Number is on file.

Vice President, Editor-in-Chief: Tim Moore
Wharton Editor: Yoram (Jerry) Wind
Editorial Assistant: Susie Abraham
Development Editor: Russ Hall
Director of Marketing: John Pierce
International Marketing Manager: Tim Galligan
Cover Designer: Chuti Prasertsith
Managing Editor: Gina Kanouse
Project Editor: Michael Thurston
Copy Editor: Gayle Johnson
Indexer: Joy Dean Lee
Compositor: The Scan Group
Proofreader: Karen A. Gill
Manufacturing Buyer: Dan Uhrig

Ideas. Action. Impact.
Wharton School
Publishing
© 2006 by Pearson Education, Inc.
Publishing as Wharton School Publishing
Upper Saddle River, New Jersey 07458

Printed in the United States of America
First Printing
This product is printed digitally on demand. This book is the paperback version
of an original hardcover book.

ISBN 0-13-248506-0

Pearson Education LTD.
Pearson Education Australia PTY, Limited.
Pearson Education Singapore, Pte. Ltd.
Pearson Education North Asia, Ltd.
Pearson Education Canada, Ltd.
Pearson Educatión de Mexico, S.A. de C.V.
Pearson Education—Japan
Pearson Education Malaysia, Pte. Ltd.

 Ideas. Action. Impact.
**Wharton School
Publishing**

Bernard Baumohl
THE SECRETS OF ECONOMIC INDICATORS
Hidden Clues to Future Economic Trends and Investment Opportunities

Sayan Chatterjee
FAILSAFE STRATEGIES
Profit and Grow from Risks That Others Avoid

Sunil Gupta, Donald R. Lehmann
MANAGING CUSTOMERS AS INVESTMENTS
The Strategic Value of Customers in the Long Run

Stuart L. Hart
CAPITALISM AT THE CROSSROADS
The Unlimited Business Opportunities in Solving the World's Most Difficult Problems

Lawrence G. Hrebiniak
MAKING STRATEGY WORK
Leading Effective Execution and Change

Robert Mittelstaedt
WILL YOUR NEXT MISTAKE BE FATAL?
Avoiding the Chain of Mistakes That Can Destroy Your Organization

Mukul Pandya, Robbie Shell, Susan Warner, Sandeep Junnarkar, Jeffrey Brown
NIGHTLY BUSINESS REPORT PRESENTS LASTING LEADERSHIP
What You Can Learn from the Top 25 Business People of Our Times

C. K. Prahalad
THE FORTUNE AT THE BOTTOM OF THE PYRAMID
Eradicating Poverty Through Profits

Arthur Rubinfeld
BUILT FOR GROWTH
Expanding Your Business Around the Corner or Across the Globe

Scott A. Shane
FINDING FERTILE GROUND
Identifying Extraordinary Opportunities for New Ventures

Oded Shenkar
THE CHINESE CENTURY
The Rising Chinese Economy and Its Impact on the Global Economy, the Balance of Power, and Your Job

David Sirota, Louis A. Mischkind, and Michael Irwin Meltzer
THE ENTHUSIASTIC EMPLOYEE
How Companies Profit by Giving Workers What They Want

Thomas T. Stallkamp
SCORE!
A Better Way to Do Busine$$: Moving from Conflict to Collaboration

Yoram (Jerry)Wind, Colin Crook, with Robert Gunther
THE POWER OF IMPOSSIBLE THINKING
Transform the Business of Your Life and the Life of Your Business

This book is dedicated to the consumers, business executives, political leaders, thought leaders, and government and nongovernment organizations who are offering solutions that make a difference to the developing countries—the 86 percent markets.

Receive Special Benefits by Registering this Book

Register this book today and receive exclusive benefits that you can't obtain anywhere else, including:

- Wharton Fellow field reports for Shanghai, Prague, and India

- The article, "The 86 Percent Opportunity," by Vijay Mahajan from the Jan-March issue of *The Smart Manager*

To register this book, use the following special code when you visit your My Account page on Whartonsp.com.

Special Code: minition9070

Note that the benefits for registering may vary from book to book. To see the benefits associated with a particular book, you must be a member and submit the book's ISBN (the ISBN is the number on the back of this book that starts with 0-13-) on the registration page.

CONTENTS

ABOUT THE AUTHORS

Vijay Mahajan, former dean of the Indian School of Business, holds the John P. Harbin Centennial Chair in Business at McCombs School of Business, University of Texas at Austin. He has received numerous lifetime achievement awards including the American Marketing Association (AMA) Charles Coolidge Parlin Award for visionary leadership in scientific marketing. The AMA also instituted the Vijay Mahajan Award in 2000 for career contributions to marketing strategy.

Mahajan is author or editor of nine books. He is one of the world's most widely cited researchers in business and economics. He edited the *Journal of Marketing Research*, and has consulted with Fortune 500 companies and delivered executive development programs worldwide.

Kamini Banga is an independent marketing consultant and managing director of Dimensions Consultancy Pvt. Ltd. Her clients have included Cadbury, Philips, Johnson & Johnson, Coca-Cola, and many others. She has traveled extensively in Asia and Southeast Asia, conducting training programs on market research and consumer behavior. During a three-year stint in London, she worked with the Harris Research Center as a consultant on ethnic issues for companies including British Airways and the BBC.

Banga writes and edits business articles for *Economic Times*, *The Smart Manager*, *Business Today*, and other leading Indian business publications, and is a non-executive director on several company boards. She is a graduate of the Indian Institute of Management, the premier institute for MBA education in India. A former resident of Mumbai, India, she now lives in London.

SEEING GEETI

As she begins her day, Geeti is amazed at how much her world has changed. She works as a customer service representative on the campus of an outsourcing company in Hi-Tech City in Hyderabad. It looks and feels more like Silicon Valley than India. She has a cell phone, a Sony television, and a Dell computer with a high-speed Internet connection that links her to relatives, information, and markets around the globe. Her Haier refrigerator hums in her 1,000-square-foot apartment. So many new products from local and global companies have flooded into the market. She has just bought her first car, settling on a well-equipped model from Maruti, costing about US$3,000 (138,000 rupees), with only US$45 (2,000 rupees) down.

She realizes that her new car won't be gliding down the smooth highways shown in the Western television commercials. It will have to navigate crowded streets and rural highways jammed with bullock carts, bicycles, scooters, pedestrians, and beggars. And her electricity is often out several hours a day as she stares at her blank computer screen in the light of battery-operated lamps. She is looking into buying an inverter (an uninterruptible, battery-like power source).

Still, this life is a far cry from the simple, rural Indian village where she grew up. That village exists only in her memory now. The other day, her older sister, Laju, who still lives there, called from a cell phone operated by a telephone lady during the weekly haat, *or market day. Hindi music from the latest Bollywood films was blaring in the background. Laju talked about the sachets of branded products crowded onto tables with traditional spices and clothing. She told how her husband, Shiv, and other rural farmers track grain prices on the Chicago Mercantile Exchange through a satellite Internet hub called e-Choupal. And she reported how her son, Anil, working in the Middle East with his wife, Sudha, deposits money in an account in Dubai that allows Laju to draw cash from an ICICI Bank mobile automatic teller in the village. Of course, Laju didn't miss this opportunity to ask her little sister again when she and her new husband are planning to have children. Geeti doesn't know how she will ever find the time.*

Geeti's maid, Lakshmi, arrives on a bicycle driven by her husband, Ghelu Mohan. They are thinking about trading up to a scooter and have asked Geeti for a recommendation. She has had a good experience with Bajaj, the brand she owned before she bought her car. Geeti bought her maid a cell phone so that she could relay messages about schedules and dinner plans. The maid and her family live in a crowded one-room shanty with no indoor plumbing, but their life is changing as well.

At the other extreme, when Geeti was chosen to accompany her supervisor to the airport to pick up a visiting client from the U.S., they rented a fully equipped Mercedes from a local company competing with Hertz. A GPS system offered directions, and the satellite radio was tuned to Western classical music on their way to the ITC Kakatia Sheraton. The air-conditioned automobile sat in traffic next to sidewalks jammed with garbage. Noisy generators were audible through the closed windows. As she looked out, Geeti saw the children of construction workers defecating in the street. She also thought about the spreading AIDS crisis sweeping Andhra Prashad, the state where Hyderabad is located, which has the highest incidence of the disease in India. The response to the crisis has brought out the best from outside and inside the country, from the initiatives of the Bill & Melinda Gates Foundation to a new Hyderabad 10k run (www.hyderabad10k.com), an idea imported from America to raise money for children's health and other causes. Even the most luxurious car could not insulate one completely from the realities of an under-developed infrastructure and society. How long would it take for India to become a developed nation?

Geeti finds herself at the center of a complex and rapidly changing world. She is part of the 86 percent of the world that has a per capita gross national product (GNP) of less than $10,000 per year. So is her sister. So are the executives driving Mercedes. These are markets that have largely been invisible to companies outside of them (and even to some firms within them), who have focused their attention on the 14 percent of the world's population in the developed world.

Not only do these 86 percent markets represent the future of global commerce, but they also present rich opportunities for com-panies that have the imagination and creativity to envision Geeti and other consumers. But you won't recognize these opportunities through the lens of the developed world. You won't reach these customers through the market strategies that work in the 14 per-cent markets. Developing markets have no smooth superhighways, no established consumer markets, no distribution networks, and, in many cases, no electricity. Developing markets are younger, behind in technology (but rapidly catching up), and inexperienced as con-sumers. These markets are very different. Yet with creative solu-tions tailored to their distinctive characteristics, as we will discuss in this book, you can realize the rich opportunities of these 86 percent markets.

Preface: Do You Want to Be in This Market? Can You Afford Not to Be?

Managers at a major U.S. office equipment manufacturer were considering how to market an overhead projector to the developing world when we asked a simple question: How would the overhead projector work without electricity? There was silence. It was a question that they had never even considered. But this is a question that must be answered every day in the developing world. By asking and answering this type of question, Hewlett-Packard has created battery-operated digital cameras and printing systems that allow entrepreneurial photographers to operate completely off the grid. Ask yourself: Do you know what an inverter is? If you don't, you probably haven't thought enough about the weak infrastructure and other distinctive conditions of emerging markets. These differences, and the strategies needed to address them, are the focus of this book.

To appreciate the complexities of these markets and solutions designed to meet their needs, consider the toilet. China is now second only to the U.S. in web users. It is expected to have more broadband and mobile-phone users than any other nation by 2006. Yet more than 60 percent of Chinese citizens do not have access to proper sanitation. This means about 700 million people in China (along with another 700 million in India) do not have a basic toilet. Think about that. Researchers at MIT's Media Lab are creating wearable computers, but wouldn't a computer built into a toilet be a more appropriate solution for the developing world? The airport in Frankfort, Germany has toilets that automatically clean their seats and flush themselves. South Korea, as the logical outcome of a national obsession with technology, has set a goal of having 10 million "smart homes" online by 2007, including toilets that relay body temperature, pulse rates, and urinalysis results to your doctor. Yet a market of more than a billion people has gone virtually unmet. Where are the innovations focused on the parts of the world that lack sanitation?

This is not about altruism. In creating solutions for the developing world, companies can solve one of the most pressing problems facing them today: sustaining growth. IBM's Global CEO Study in 2004 found that four out of five CEOs believe that revenue growth is the most important path to boosting financial performance.[1] Where will this growth come from? With the largest populations and fastest growth rates on the planet, developing markets represent the future of the global economy. To seize the opportunities of these 86 percent markets, we need different mind-sets and market strategies. We need managers who can envision creating a business selling sachets of shampoo for pennies, distributing products in stores the size of phone booths, or offering credit cards to people whose idea of banking is storing rolls of coins in a money belt. As you will see in the following pages, the creative companies that serve these markets are willing to provide refrigeration along with their bottles of cola and design cars that are modeled after bullock carts. They can sell a product to a customer in California that is picked up by a relative in Mexico City. In short, they have used a distinctive set of market strategies to recognize and realize the opportunities of these 86 percent markets.

This book is designed to challenge the thinking of managers from developed markets about strategies that have worked well in the past. Managers in developing countries will find some new insights from different parts of the developing world that will very likely work in their region. Entrepreneurs will see the rich opportunities in the emerging world. Finally, leaders of governments, nongovernmental organizations (NGOs), and other organizations can gain insights into the dynamics of business in this environment.

This book started with a phone call to Vijay in the mid-1990s from Wharton Professor Jerry Wind, who had been contacted by the organizers of a conference at the United Nations. They were looking for creative strategies to encourage developing nations to stand on their own two feet rather than relying on handouts from the developed world. The question was insulting. Many hugely successful companies have grown up in these developing nations. Entrepreneurship is alive and well. While well-meaning people in developed countries were discussing foreign aid, industrious citizens of the developing world have left their homelands for jobs in the developed world and were already sending billions of dollars back home. How could these compassionate and intelligent people from the developed world not see this?

After this discussion, Vijay, Jerry, and Marcos V. Pratini de Moraes, then minister of agriculture for Brazil, joined in writing an article on principles for reaching the forgotten 86 percent of the world in "The Invisible Global Market,"[2] published in 2000 in *Marketing Management*. Vijay continued to study this topic at the University of Texas at Austin and as dean of the Indian School of Business in Hyderabad, writing a second article on "The 86 Percent Opportunity" in India.[3] He spoke with executives and government officials in several developing countries. The growing interest in these ideas was so encouraging that he decided to work with Kamini on this book. As a consultant, Kamini is in direct contact with diverse businesses in India that are applying new strategies for these developing markets. We have seen firsthand the creative strategies they are using.

Around the same time that we were engaged in this work, C.K. Prahalad and others were focusing attention on the same areas of the world from a different perspective. In his insightful work *The Fortune at the Bottom of the Pyramid*, he points out the potential of the poorest citizens of the world. But the poorest of the poor are just one segment of these markets. Will you know how to meet the needs of the growing middle class or luxury segments? In 2004, a single Rolls Royce was sold in India for more than $700,000, some 1,500 times the average per capita gross national income in that country. This book focuses on the entire spectrum of business opportunities in these emerging markets, for both very poor and more affluent consumers. It also discusses the characteristics of these markets that must be addressed in market strategies.

In addition to the specific strategies explored in this book, we hope the examples in the following chapters will encourage you to think more broadly about the approaches that might work in your part of the world. Every day, innovative companies are coming up with new ways to address or overleap the limitations and respond to the distinctive needs of emerging markets. They are developing the 86 percent solutions. Challenge your thinking, and you can do the same.

Vijay Mahajan, Austin, Texas

Kamini Banga, London

Notes

1 "Your Turn." The Global CEO Study 2004, IBM Business Consulting Services, IBM Corporation, 2004.

2 Vijay Mahajan, Marcos V. Pratini de Moraes, and Yoram Wind. "The Invisible Global Market: Strategies for Reaching the Forgotten 86 Percent of the World." *Marketing Management*, Winter 2000, pp. 31–35.

3 Mahajan, Vijay, "The 86% Opportunity," *The Smart Manager*, Quarter 1 (2003) 17-25. Reproduced in *Business Today*, (India), Collector's Edition, 4 (2003) 50-58.

ACKNOWLEDGMENTS

We are very grateful to the many individuals who contributed insights and information or took the time to be interviewed for this book. Without their involvement and detailed knowledge, we could not have offered insights and examples from so many diverse parts of the globe.

We are indebted to so many people who contributed directly or indirectly to the ideas of this book that it is impossible to make a complete list, but we would like to acknowledge a few of the people who contributed to the success of this project. Many senior executives of companies and organizations generously offered their time and insights, including Aman Mehta of HSBC; Alex Kuruvilla of MTV India; Hemant Luthra, Rajesh Jejurikar, and P Rajendran of Mahindra & Mahindra; Suvalaxmi Chakraborty, Lalita Gupte, Nachiket Mor, Arnab Basu, and Manmeet Singh and Madhav Kalyan of ICICI Bank; Elsen Karstad of Chardust Ltd.; Sarvesh Swarup of CITI Group, India; Gautam Kumra of McKinsey, India; Sumanta Dutta of Coca Cola, China; Roger H. Steadman of the Steadman

Group; Satya Prabhakar of Sulekha.com; Partha Rakshit of AC
Nielsen, India; Indian economist Dr. Siddarth Roy; Businessworld's
Indrajit Gupta and journalist Jehangir Pocha; Alok Kejriwal and
Gopalkrishnan of contest2win; Sonal Jain of CLSA; Rajiv Dubey of
Tata Motors; Chris Callen of DHL, India; Tushar Shinde of Carrier
Aircon Ltd.; Pakistan Oil Company Managing Director Tariq
Kirmani; Mohamud Yunnus of Grameen Bank; Ashok Alexander of
the Gates Foundation in India; Manoj Kumar of the Naandi
Foundation; Vijay Mahajan of Basix, Dr. P. C. Reddy and Sangita
Reddy of Apollo Hospitals, as well as Dr. Anji Reddy of Dr. Reddy's
Labs, and Ramlinga Raju of Satyam Computer; and Drs. Srinagi and
Ramesh Babu of Medwin Hospitals; Fadi Ghandour of Aramex;
Gilberto Gonzalez Ortiz of Grupo Bimbo; and Kavita Vamuri, for-
merly of 3M-Austin.

From Unilever, we appreciated the insights and support of Vindi
Banga, President, Foods; Sanjiv Mehta, CEO of Bangladesh; and
Musharaf Hai, CEO of Pakistan; as well as the assistance of Damodar
Mall, Rahul Welde, CR Sunderrajan, Sharat Dhall, Satyendu
Krishna, Piyush Jain, Ashok Ganapathy, Donald Hepburn, Arnaz
Bhiwandiwala, and Samir Singh of Hindustan Lever Limited;
Ishmael Yamson of Unilever, Ghana; Alan Brown of Unilever, China;
and Doug Baillie of Unilever, Africa.

We are also thankful for the insights of so many friends in
Hyderabad, including Chandra Babu Naidu, former chief minister of
Andhra Pradesh, and his wife Mrs. Bhuvaneshwari Devi,; and Preeti
and Randeep Sudan of the government of Andhra Pradesh.

We are grateful to many colleagues, including Jianmin Jia of
Chinese University of Hong Kong; Ravi Shankar Kolathur of the
Indian School of Business; Romana Khan, Bin Gu, Kerem Tomak,
Genaro Gutierrez, Dae-Yong Ahn, and others from the University
of Texas at Austin. We also benefited from the insights of the

Executive Board and colleagues of the Indian School of Business, in particular. Finally, we would like to thank Roberto Gomez Salazar, Dr. Jaime Alonso Gómez, Salvador Treviño, Myrna Marquez, and Leslie Chavarria of Escuela de Graduados en Administración y Dirección de Empresas—EGADE Tecnológico de Monterrey. We also would like to thank students from Vijay's Invisible Global Markets second-year MBA marketing course at the University of Texas, who offered many valuable insights and corrections.

Many people helped guide these ideas into print. Jerry Wind was a collaborator on Vijay's first article on this topic and, as co-editor of Wharton School Publishing, is largely responsible for encouraging us to expand these ideas into a book. We would like to thank Dr. Gita Piramal, who solicited and published Vijay's second article, "The 86 Percent Opportunity," in *The Smart Manager,* which helped to clarify our thinking about this topic. Finally, Wharton School Publishing editor Tim Moore has lent his enthusiasm and insights to developing this project, also with insightful editorial comments from Charles Decker and Bob Wallace, among others.

Vijay's assistants, Diane Thompson of the University of Texas at Austin and May Philips of the Indian School of Business, offered indefatigable support in helping us make our way through countless articles and drafts.

Finally, we would like to thank our families for their tolerance and support of this project.

1

The Lands of Opportunity

The rapid development of the 86 percent of the world population in countries with a per capita gross national product (GNP) of less than $10,000 has made these areas the new lands of opportunity. But their complexity and distinctive characteristics will require different market strategies to realize these opportunities.

With growth slow at home, Procter & Gamble (P&G) stormed out of Cincinnati to increase its presence in India in 2004, slashing prices on detergents, shampoos, and other products. Unilever's Hindustan Lever, which had been in a much smaller and quieter Indian market since it first entered in 1888, responded aggressively. Prices on some products dropped by as much as half. Unilever, like other companies with small domestic markets, had a long presence in the developing world, but P&G and other U.S. firms had focused on the large and attractive at home or high-end segments abroad. P&G and many other companies were now waking up to the broader opportunities in India, China, Russia, and other developing markets. But they could not capture these opportunities with the same strategies used in developed markets. They needed new solutions.

Why the sudden interest? The US$10 billion Indian market for "fast-moving" consumer goods is expected to double in the next decade. Even if this revenue comes in a rupee at a time (about 2 U.S. cents)—the price of a sachet of detergent—the market cannot be ignored. While selling shampoo and detergent for pennies may seem like a distraction from big-ticket items of developed markets, these sachets account for more than US$1 billion in annual sales in India for Hindustan Lever alone.

In China, retail sales have increased about 15 percent annually over the past 20 years, reaching $628 billion in 2004, making it the third-largest retail market in the world. While the US$47 billion Chinese market for packaged foods is growing at 8 percent per year, Nestlé was the only major global brand among the top five packaged foods companies in China in 2003. (The others were Ting Sin and Uni-President Enterprises from Taiwan, followed by Hai Pa Wang International Food and Long Fong, with Nestlé bringing up the rear. These may not be familiar brands today, but who had heard of Haier or Lenovo a decade ago?)

Emerging Markets Start Their Engines

HIS **FIRST** GRAND PRIX.
AND A BILLION FANS ALREADY!

(Courtesy of Saatchi & Saatchi)

Youthful markets and rising automobile ownership have made racing a growing sport in developing countries. In addition to the Olympics in Beijing, Shanghai hosted its first Formula One Grand Prix race in late 2004, perhaps the first ever in a developing country. China spent more than $300 million for the rights to host the race and the construction of a new track with 200,000 seats. It is shaped like the Chinese character *shang*, which stands for "high" or "upward." The race was carried for three days on Chinese national television, sponsored by state oil company Sinopec and international companies such as Mobil and Toyota. Meanwhile, youthful Indian Formula One driver Narain Karthikeyan dominated front-page news during the Australian Formula One race in March 2005. Karthikeyan already has a billion fans, which is a boon for sponsors such as Bharat Petroleum's, Tata Motors, and tire maker Bridgestone (see ad above). The Iranian woman driver Laleh Seddigh has become a celebrity and symbol of change by racing fans across cultural and gender lines. Racing is so popular in developing countries that it has spawned the creation of a new rival to Formula One. Backed by a member of Dubai's ruling family, the new A1 Grand Prix has invited 25 countries—including Mexico, Brazil, Lebanon, Pakistan, South Africa, and China—to field one team each, with races scheduled during Formula One's off-season. While only a small percentage of the population of the 86 percent economies can afford automobiles, these markets are clearly revving their engines.

Markets for scooters, cars, refrigerators, beer, and many other products in developing countries are heating up. Shanghai hosted its first Formula One Grand Prix race in 2004—a sign of growing interest in the sport across the developing world (see sidebar). The "consumer class" (defined as people with incomes of greater than $7,000 in purchasing power parity) has an estimated 1.7 billion members throughout the world. Nearly half of them live in the developing world. By this measure, these consumers include more than 240 million in China, only slightly below the 270 million members of the consumer class in the U.S., and 120 million in India, equivalent to the consumer class in Japan. In fact, the size of this consumer class in China and India alone is greater than in all of Western Europe (although their spending power is certainly not as great).

These developing-world numbers are growing very rapidly. By 2003, China had more than 10 million private cars, including more than 1 million in Beijing alone. In China, a quarter of the population owns color televisions (more than 300 million), and more than 16 percent (more than 200 million) have mobile phones. Companies from countries such as Japan, China, Korea, India, Brazil, and Turkey are now dominating markets in the developing nations. In India, Samsung, LG, and Hyundai have each notched up sales of about $1 billion in the past decade. These companies from the developing world understand from their own experience what it takes to meet the needs of these markets.

While major developing nations such as China and India are now clearly on the radar screens of global companies, some firms have had a very difficult time capitalizing on the apparent opportunities. They have launched products and pulled back, changed their branding, or seen their positions undermined by local rivals. Multinational cell phone companies in China initially focused on the big cities, but Chinese firms such as Ningbo Bird and TCL ran circles around them by targeting the rural areas and designing for local tastes, taking half the market. (The global players, smarting from the hard knocks, have shifted their strategies dramatically and are winning back market share.) Beermakers in China and other developing markets saw their seasoned global brands go flat in the face of scrappy local rivals. What these companies learned the hard way is that the 86 percent markets behave differently from the 14 percent markets of developed nations. Developing markets may be the new lands of opportunity, but do you have the right market strategies to reach them?

The 86 Percent Opportunity

For generations, the developed world has been seen as the land of opportunity. Immigrants crowded into ships or trucks to cross into the land of promise. Companies poured their resources into serving these populations. Developed markets have high incomes and well-developed infrastructures, so it is no wonder that the developed world is where most companies have devoted the lion's share of their attention, and they are still attractive markets. But now these developed markets represent a shrinking part of the world market. Just 14 percent of the world's more than 6 billion people live in countries with a per capita GNP of greater than US$10,000 (see Figure 1-1). Kenichi Ohmae has called this cutoff for developed nations "the $10,000 club," although there are diverse definitions of developing countries (see the sidebar).[1] Yet the developed world is where most companies have concentrated their resources, based on essentially the same argument that Willie Sutton used to explain why he robbed banks—because that was where the money was. The rest of the world, 86 percent of the population, was deemed too poor or too far away to matter. But this is no longer true, and it becomes less so every day.

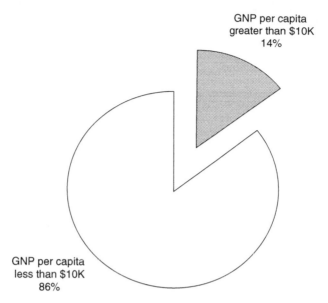

FIGURE 1-1 While many companies have focused on developed markets, 86 percent of the world population is in developing countries with a GNP per capita of less than $10,000. This percentage will continue to increase in the coming decades.

When Do Emerging Markets Emerge?

Although the $10,000 GNP per capita is a convenient cutoff, there are many definitions for emerging or developing countries. Some have used membership in the Organization for Economic Cooperation and Development (OECD) as a sign of development, but the OECD includes countries such as Turkey, Mexico, and Poland that are usually classified as emerging. Other systems, such as a list from *The Economist*, use more fluid classifications that place countries such as Hong Kong or Singapore in the emerging world despite relatively high incomes. Some assessments are based on purchase power parity (PPP). In drawing the line between the developed and developing world, we have chosen the $10,000 GNP per capita cutoff, identified by Kenichi

Ohmae as a significant milestone in national development because of the real implications for disposable income and market development. This is not to ignore the substantial variations and distinctive characteristics of countries that might share a similar GNP per capita.

We Can't Wait for Them to "Grow Up"

Doesn't it make sense to wait for these developing nations to become developed before pursuing them? The risks will be reduced, and we will have business problems that we know how to solve. At that point, these populations will have enough disposable income and mature infrastructures to make it possible to easily create profitable businesses based on models from other developed nations. But we can't wait. It will take too long. How many companies have become developed nations in the past 50 years? How many will become developed in the next 20 years? Excluding Japan, only a handful of countries with relatively small populations have become developed since the 1970s, including Israel, Singapore, Taiwan, Kuwait, Ireland, and possibly South Korea. Not a single developed nation exists in South America or Africa, and Asia has only a few. It took Japan more than 27 years to advance from a per capita GNP of less than $1,000 to reach the $10,000 club. Although other countries aspire to follow this example, one wonders how many of them will be able to achieve the phenomenal growth needed to join this club in the next two decades.

By 2020, in China and India only an estimated 5 percent of the population will have a per capita GNP of more than $10,000. As shown in Figure 1-2, many countries have a long way to travel before they reach the $10,000 mark. Assuming a constant growth rate of 5.5 percent, it would take India almost 60 years to enter the $10,000 club.

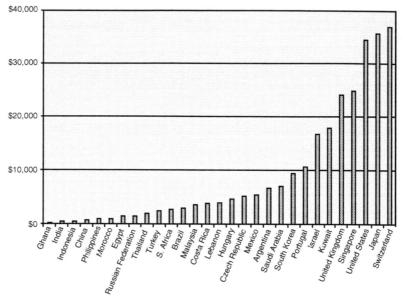

FIGURE 1-2   Although they are growing rapidly, many developing countries, particularly the most populous ones, have a long way to go to enter the "$10,000 club." (Source: World Bank, World Development Report, 2003, GNI per capita for 2001)

During this time, fortunes will be created or lost, and companies and brands will be built or destroyed. In the long run, these emerging economies will be developed nations, but as economist John Maynard Keynes observed, "In the long run, we are all dead."[2] We cannot kid ourselves that we can wait for these markets to mature.

These Markets Contain Entire "Developed Nations" Today

Even though development will be slow, given the sheer size of populations of developing markets, there may soon be more rich people in the 86 percent markets than in the 14 percent markets. For example, if just a little less than 6 percent of the developing world achieved the $10,000 per capita GNP mark, this would represent a population of more than 350 million, greater than the size of the entire U.S.

These Markets Are Where the Growth Is

As consumer markets and economies expand, companies such General Electric are staking their future on the developing world (see the following sidebar). These companies recognize that this is where the growth is. While developed countries posted GNP growth rates of less than 3 percent from 1980 to 1995, developing countries averaged almost 6 percent growth in the same period. The U.S. still accounts for about a third of the global GDP, but its growth is slower than the developing world—about 3 percent. China's aggregate GNP has grown about 10 percent per year since the late 1970s, and India has been posting about 6 percent annual growth since 1991.[3] The sheer size of populations in the developing world should give companies pause. They represent more than 5 billion of the 6 billion people in the world and are expected to grow to more than 6 billion of 7 billion in the next two decades. Remove Japan, the U.S., and the European Union, and less than 2 percent of the world's population is in other developed markets.

Finding Growth in a Slow-Growth World

General Electric, which was a pioneer in developing Indian outsourcing and technology businesses under CEO Jack Welch, now sees the developing world as a key driver for its future growth. As its 2004 annual report noted, "We have prepared to make our own growth in a slow-growth world . . . Global revenues grew 18% and reached $72 billion in 2004. The most exciting global opportunities for GE are in the developing world, where our 2004 revenues were $21 billion, a 37% increase . . . We believe that 60% of our growth will come from developing countries in the next decade versus about 20% for the past 10 years. It is important for us to understand future customers, suppliers, and competitors in these regions, where we believe GE has a meaningful competitive advantage."[3]

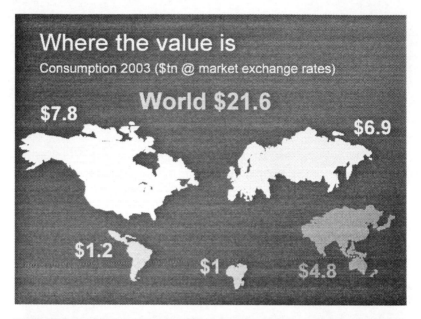

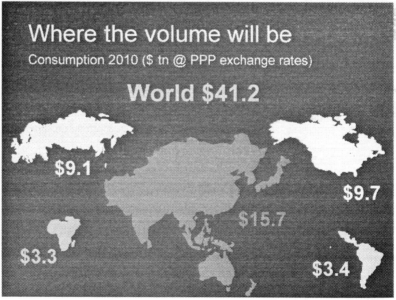

FIGURE 1-3   As global consumption rises from $14 trillion to $21 trillion between 2003 and 2010, the center will shift from North America to Asia and other parts of the developing world. (Source: Donald Hepburn, Unilever, 2004)

These developing markets have consumers spending real money today, and with more on the way. Large populations and high growth rates translate into rapidly growing markets, as shown in Figure 1-3. An estimated 35 to 40 percent of profits among the U.S. companies on Standard & Poor's 500-stock index come from outside the U.S. Despite anti-American sentiment after the launch of the Iraq war, U.S. companies earned profits of $102 billion from overseas affiliates in the first half of 2004, up 38 percent from the year before. Goldman Sachs estimates that in less than four decades, the combined GDP of Brazil, Russia, India, and China (the "BRIC economies") could be larger than the G6 in U.S. dollar terms. Of the top six countries based on GDP, only the U.S. and Japan would remain on the G6 list by 2050.[4]

These Markets Are the Future

As developing markets experience rapid growth in populations and income, they are becoming more central to defining the future in many industries. They are now helping shape technology standards and are playing a growing role in culture and entertainment. For example, Bollywood in India releases nearly 1,200 movies per year, compared to 450 for Hollywood. Indian box offices sell 12 million tickets per day. The arrival of the musical *Bombay Dreams* on Broadway in April 2004 (despite its questionable financial performance) is a further sign of what the show's coproducer, Bollywood director-producer Shekhar Kapur, calls a process of "reverse cultural colonization." Kapur foresees the day, not too far off, when Spiderman will remove his mask to reveal an Indian or Chinese face. (Already a comic-book version of the arachnid superhero story has been released, set in Mumbai with an Indian hero.) This view may be shocking to folks in the insular world of Hollywood, but it's not at all surprising from the perspective of Bollywood. The success of films from China, such as *Hero* and *Crouching Tiger, Hidden Dragon,* which grossed $128 million in U.S. markets, also indicates the emergence of new centers of filmmaking. Some 600 international film festivals take place each year in the world, many of them in the developing world.

It is not just the faces that are changing, but also the themes. While Hollywood may make movies like *Waterworld* and *The Day After Tomorrow*, envisioning a time when the Earth is covered with water, Bollywood is focusing more on developing-world themes. In the movie *Water*, for example, factions in a futuristic city battle over scarce water supplies in India. In the 2004 Indian movie *Swades* ("We, the People"), Shah Rukh Khan stars as a NASA engineer who returns to a rural Indian village, working to improve the electricity and water supplies, living in an RV stocked with bottled water and a satellite connection to the Internet—a home on wheels with all the modern facilities that the village lacked. These films are very much grounded in the realities of the developing world. To understand where the world is headed, companies need to have a presence in this world.

If You Can Make It Here, You Can Make It Anywhere

According to the popular Frank Sinatra song, New York used to be the proving ground for individuals and companies. But the companies that have cut their teeth on the challenging markets of the developing world have often found ways to export their solutions to the rest of the 86 percent market and even to the 14 percent populations of the developed world.

TCL came out of China to become the largest television manufacturer in the world, purchasing the venerable RCA brand in 2003 to create a $3.5 billion company with factories in China, Vietnam, the Philippines, and Germany. In December 2004, Chinese computer maker Lenovo (formerly Legend) bought a majority stake in IBM's PC business for $1.75 billion in cash and stock, making it the third-largest PC maker in the world and giving it control of the IBM ThinkPad brand. IBM retains a minority stake in the merged company. The US$600 million in cash that IBM took from the deal is insignificant, representing less than 1 percent of the company's US$89 billion 2003 revenue. But the move positions IBM's brand for growth in China and the rest of the world, with an on-the-ground partner in the world's fastest-growing market for PCs.

Appliance manufacturer Haier, in just two decades, went from having a single plant in China to become the second-largest refrigerator maker in the world and a fixture in college dorm rooms in the developed world. Mexican cement company Cemex, after meeting the tough logistical challenges of its home market, has risen to become the world's third-largest cement maker with operations in more than 30 countries. Turkish conglomerate Koc Group, which offers products and services from appliances to financial services, posted 2003 revenues of more than $11 billion. More than 45 percent of these revenues were drawn from international sales, fueled by purchases of local brands in Germany, Austria, Romania, and other parts of the world. Brazilian aircraft manufacturer Embraer became the world's fourth-largest commercial aircraft manufacturer and Brazil's second-largest exporter in 2004.

The solutions to the challenges of these demanding environments lead to products that are cheaper and better. Brands that have built a broad base of support in the developing world can use this momentum to enter developed markets.

Opportunities at Many Levels

One of the dangers of talking about the "developing world" or even the "86 percent markets" is that it may seem to imply that a monolithic market opportunity exists. Nothing could be further from the truth. It is overly simplistic to focus on only the very poor or luxury segments of these markets. There is, in fact, a continuum of segments—all of which are moving rapidly upward. The 86 percent market represents a patchwork of very different markets, across countries and within countries, as can be seen in the demand for vehicles from bicycles to automobiles.

Bicycles, Motorcycles, and Automobiles

The head of Daimler Chrysler in India sold just one dozen Mercedes SL500s in 2003, priced around 8.2 million rupees each (US$179,000) That's an average of just one car per month, but he considers that a good year. At the same time, companies such as Tata Motors are finding opportunities by working with scooter designers to develop an automobile with a remarkable price tag of about $2,000 to make it easy for motorcycle owners to trade up.

But even automobiles do not represent the full spectrum of the market. Some 76 percent of the 40 million vehicles on Indian roads are not cars at all, but two-wheelers, including motorcycles, scooters, and bicycles (see Figure 1-4). Two-wheelers, considered "family vehicles," are cheaper than cars and cost less to run. While slightly less than 1 million passenger vehicles were sold in India in 2003–2004, more than 5.6 million two-wheelers were sold in the same period.[5] Why is all the media attention focused on the automobile industry in the developing world?

**Market Share
2003-2004**

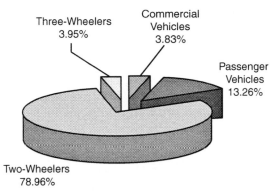

FIGURE 1-4 A large market rides on two wheels. (Source: Indian Automobile Manufacturers, 2004)

Bicycles represent a large part of this two-wheeled market, which is dominated by companies from developing markets. China is the world's largest producer of bicycles. It exports 500,000 bicycles per year to the European Union. Other major bicycle producers come from countries such as India, Vietnam, and Poland. Companies in these countries understand that two-wheeled transportation means something different from the X Games and the Tour de France.

Is focusing on these low-priced two-wheelers worth it? By meeting the needs of this two-wheeler market, Hero Group in India has become the world's largest manufacturer of bicycles and created one of the top brands in India. Its Hero Honda partnership with Japan's Honda Motor Company has become the world's largest manufacturer of two-wheelers, particularly motorcycles. By 2003, Hero Group sales surpassed $1.8 billion, roughly equivalent to the global sales of Pier 1 Imports (801 on the 2003 Fortune 1000 list). Hero has put more than 55 million bicycles and 7 million motorcycles on

Indian roads. While car companies were slowly building their businesses in India and China, Hero Group in India rode its humble two-wheelers to 29 percent compound annual growth in revenues and 40 percent compound annual growth in profits between 1998 and 2003. For 2002–2003, it posted nearly 46 percent return on equity. Hero now exports bicycles, cycle components, motorcycles, mopeds, and castings to more than 70 countries and also has branched into services.

Diverse Segments

As the market for vehicles illustrates, developing markets have diverse segments:

- **The rich and super-rich**—In 2004, a Beijing man paid $215,000 in an auction for the ultimate lucky cell phone number (133-3333-3333). Although the buyer was not identified, even the developing world clearly has people with money to burn. The 2004 *Forbes* list of billionaires included newcomers from Kazakhstan, Poland, and Ukraine, and Indian steel baron Lakshmi Mittal moved into third place behind Bill Gates and Warren Buffet. While an estimated 400 million Chinese live on less than $2 per day, *Asia Money* estimates that 50,000 Chinese have fortunes of more than $10 million. Although nearly half of Mexico's citizens live in poverty, that country had more than 85,000 millionaires in 2004, more billionaires than Saudi Arabia, Switzerland, and Taiwan. Most of Vietnam consists of poor rural areas, but World Bank economists estimate that the average household of four people in Ho Chi Minh City or Hanoi spent the equivalent of $20,000 in 2002 (based on purchasing power parity). It is no wonder that Louis Vuitton tripled its floor space in Hanoi in 2004. In the two decades since the first Chinese golf course was established in 1984, more than 200 have been constructed on the mainland, a figure expected to double in the next decade. Even a luxury yacht factory has set up shop in China, although the domestic market may be years away from emerging. Yet the Mercedes and Bentleys of the developing world are rolling out onto muddy country roads that are often choked with other traffic. Automakers also had to add lights and air conditioning to the backseat because, with low labor costs, these cars are usually chauffer-driven.

- **The middle class**—Sales of consumer durables, cars, and mobile telephones are growing as the disposable incomes and aspirations in emerging markets surge upward. In 2003, the Chinese Academy of Social Sciences concluded that the middle class accounted for 19 percent of China's 1.3 billion population in 2003, nearly 250 million, and it was expected to rise to 40 percent by 2020. The middle class in China could surpass the middle class in the U.S. within a decade or two. (While other estimates were lower, all indicate that there is a significant and growing middle class.) For this segment, the price-value equation is the most critical factor. The Housing Development Finance Corporation Ltd. (HDFC), founded by Hasmukhbhai Parekh, became India's top housing finance company by offering loans at minimal rates with low down payments. This made it possible for people to dream of owning their first homes. These growing middle-class markets also have driven demand for automobiles, appliances, student loans, and many other products.

- **The poor**—About 1.1 billion people in developing countries live on an income of less than $1 per day, including one-third of the population of India and Brazil. Rapid economic growth in East and South Asia has helped decrease the number of people living in extreme poverty from 40 percent of the global population in 1981 to 21 percent in 2001. However, the very poor still represent a significant portion of developing markets. Contrary to popular perceptions, these low-income segments still consume products such as potable water, electricity, tea, low-cost laundry detergents, toothpaste, transportation, and communication services. Although prices and margins are low, large numbers can make these very profitable markets, particularly for products that address people's pressing needs. There are strong opportunities to build markets among the poor, as C.K. Prahalad has demonstrated in *The Fortune at the Bottom of the Pyramid*.

- **The rural**—By 2004, it was estimated that rural India's share in total consumption of fast-moving consumer goods (such as toothpaste, cream, and food products) and consumer durables exceeded urban India's share. A study in smaller towns of India suggested that revenues from rural STD and ISD (booths offering domestic and international phone calls) are greater than for larger towns. Different rural segments present different opportunities. For example, the rich farmer is a good potential market for farm equipment, transport for rural roads, TV sets, consumer durables, gensets (generator sets), and cell phones. There is a need for low-cost housing and information on weather, daily crop prices, and availability of raw materials and other products. Globally, areas known as "teledeserts" are beginning to blossom with high-speed satellite links. Bedouin nomads in the Middle East negotiate deals for their sheep and goats on cell phones. In the West African countries of Ivory Coast and Ghana, shared cell phones are enabling rural coffee and cocoa farmers to call produce markets in the cities and negotiate their own prices. While it can be a daunting task to reach these markets, companies are beginning to unlock their potential.

Companies have built successful businesses by catering to the poorest of the poor, by offering luxury products to the rich, or anywhere in between. Yet all these segments share a common environment and characteristics that shape the opportunities of developing markets. These distinctive characteristics, as summarized next, are the focus of the market strategies discussed throughout this book.

Characteristics of Emerging Markets and the Opportunities They Create

Each of the specific differences in developing markets presents challenges for companies entering these markets but also creates opportunities for companies with the right solutions.

Characteristic #1: Markets and Culture Are Demanding

Dust and heat, lack of electricity, narrow highways, and low budgets all place strains on products in the developing world. While companies might be tempted to produce second-rate products for the developing world, consumers are very demanding, expecting high value for their scarce cash. Products and services also have to be adapted to local cultures and traditions, which can be very different from those in the developed world. How do you sell jewelry and clothing in Islamic countries, which do not allow you to show women's faces? How do you sell food and beauty products to a market that is concerned about their being *halal*? Customers in these markets also have not yet developed a culture of consumerism. They don't know how to be customers, so strategies used in developed markets, such as money-back guarantees, can have unexpected effects. The *memsahib* (Indian housewife) and other social networks can have a major impact on the growth of products, brands, and markets.

> Opportunity: By adapting to different cultures, rugged environments, and demanding price-performance targets, companies can develop breakthrough designs for product and service offerings. Sometimes these solutions may look more like a motorized "bullock cart" than a traditional automobile. From meeting the demand for *halal* foods to offering Islamic banking services and cell phones that

point the way to Mecca, companies can reach a Muslim market that accounts for one in five customers in developing markets. How do you need to modify or create products and services designed for the local conditions of developing markets? How can you build consumerism and use social networks to build markets for your products?

Characteristic #2: There Are High Rates of Emigration to the Developed World

The developing world is exporting not only products and services to the developed world, but also people. The foreign-born population in the U.S. rose to 31 million people in the last census in 2000, up 57 percent from 1990. These immigrants are in touch with family and friends back home. Globally, immigrants sent home an estimated $93 billion in 2003, second only to foreign direct investment as the largest financial flow from the developed to the developing world. While immigrants are formally a part of developed markets, they are part of something much bigger. These global diasporas are redefining the borders of markets and creating social networks that stretch across the developed and developing world.

Opportunity: By understanding the global social networks of immigrants and their friends and family back home, companies can draw on the resources of the developed world to meet the needs of end users in the developing world. Companies can develop "bank shots" to sell products that are paid for in the U.S. but delivered to relatives in Mexico or India. Companies also can serve immigrants abroad and create services to weave together the far-flung networks of this "ricochet economy." How can you build businesses across these global social networks?

Characteristic #3: Markets Are Fragmented

Developing markets are highly fragmented, with few national brands that have a commanding presence. For example, beer companies initially saw China as a huge monolithic market waiting to be tapped with their global megabrands. After the first push failed, however, it became clear that this market would be won one local market at a time. Local beers were thriving, and large companies began to acquire them. In the words of Wai Kee Tan, vice president for corporate affairs in Asia for Belgian-based Interbrew SA, "China is a nation, but not a national market."[6] MTV and HSBC have succeeded by making their global brands local, market by market around the world. Branding strategies and portfolios need to be tailored to the reality of fragmented, market-stall economies.

> Opportunity: By developing or acquiring strong local brands and tailoring global brands to local markets, companies can tap into the power of regional communities. They can leverage their global brands and capture the imagination of the local market. What is the right balance of global and local brands needed to connect with the market?

Characteristic #4: Populations Are Youthful and Growing

While Japan, Europe, and the U.S. are worried about pensions and the rapid aging of their populations, emerging economies are young. Peter Drucker has declared that the "youth market is over,"[7] but in the developing world, the youth market is just beginning. While only 21 percent of the U.S. population is under the age of 14, this figure is 33 percent in India, 29 percent in Brazil, and 33 percent in Iran (and remember, these percentages are on a much larger population base). Most of the world's population growth will take place in developing countries.

Opportunity: A young population creates markets for education, games, entertainment, apparel, fast foods, cafes, fashion, magazines and books, beauty products, music, and other products and services. While young people are globally attuned, the youth in developing markets can be different from those in the developed world, and companies need to be aware of the pushback from tradition. By thinking young, companies can connect with these burgeoning youth markets. How can you create the offerings and positioning to reach these youthful markets?

Characteristic #5: There Is Limited Income and Space

Incomes and cash flows in the developing world are much lower. In rural and poor segments, low income limits purchases. But even in more affluent sectors, there is a tendency to limit purchase size. In environments of past or present scarcity, cash is kept liquid rather than being tied up in household inventory. Saving rates in China and nine other rapidly developing countries climbed from 20 percent to 34 percent between the early 1970s and early 1990s, at the same time that savings in industrialized countries fell. While consumers are buying "super size" or "economy size" in the developed world, sachets of shampoo and other products are accounting for billions of dollars of revenue in the developing world. In the developed world, customers pay a premium for convenience. In the developing world, customers buy small for different reasons. Homes are much smaller, so furnishings and other products need to be scaled accordingly. India, with 342 people per square kilometer, is more than 11 times as densely populated as the U.S. (31), and China is more than four and a half times as densely populated (135).

Opportunity: By reducing package size, offering small payments, using demand pooling, and tailoring products to small spaces, companies can build billion-dollar markets a few pennies at a time. Like the just-in-time inventory systems of Toyota or Dell, companies need to design systems to help consumers fill their "just-in-time pantries." How can you grow a large business by thinking small payments, packages, and products?

Characteristic #6: Infrastructure Is Weak

Most of the rural population of the 86 percent markets is inaccessible by motor vehicles, and they lack good sanitation and electricity. At the same time, the cities are growing very rapidly, and this fast urbanization has placed tremendous strains on the urban infrastructure. Infrastructure everywhere in the developing world is fragile or underdeveloped. Transportation networks are nonexistent. Power failures are frequent. Clean water and sanitation are often lacking. Underdeveloped economic systems and restrictive regulations have created thriving informal or parallel economies in developing nations. It is estimated that the informal economy accounts for at least 40 percent of the GNP of low-income nations.

Opportunity: The weak infrastructure creates opportunities for companies that can fill the gaps with water purification systems, generators, inverters, and other products. It also creates opportunities for companies that can find ways to work around holes in the infrastructure, such as through ready-to-eat meals that don't require refrigeration. The informal economy may present opportunities for legitimate businesses. How can you find opportunities in the holes in the infrastructure?

Characteristic #7: Technology Is Underdeveloped

The developed world has had a head start of many decades in land-line telephones, computing, and other technologies. The developed world has had a much longer time to build technology-intensive industries such as pharmaceuticals and biotechnology, with the support of academic institutions and supplier networks. How could developing countries ever hope to compete? Won't the market for technology be slow to develop in the 86 percent world?

> Opportunity: Powerful new technologies can leap across the boundaries of the developing world. Without the constraints of legacy systems, companies have opportunities to create new systems from scratch, often leapfrogging old technology. Technology can spread very rapidly as consumers quickly adopt it without the switching costs of developed-market customers. How you create the technologies, or ride the technologies, to allow your business to leapfrog with the market?

Characteristic #8: Distribution Channels Are Weak

Developing nations have poor distribution systems. In large cities, distribution is often through small, hole-in-the-wall shops such as the *paanwalla* shops in India, the *tiendas de la esquinas* in Mexico, and *sari-sari* stores in the Philippines. A market of 600 million is locked in India's villages, 42 percent of which have populations of less than 500, with weak connections to the outside world. The lack of media, roadways, and electricity creates seemingly impenetrable barriers. Some villages don't have retail outlets at all, and some distribution opportunities, such as market days or carnivals, are temporary in nature.

> Opportunity: By building distribution or utilizing the existing idiosyncratic systems in the developing world, such as small shops and market days, companies can find ways to

"take the market to the people," meeting the diffused and fragmented markets of the developing world where they live. How can you create the distribution networks to reach the dispersed markets of developing countries?

Characteristic #9: Markets Are Changing Rapidly

By definition, the global 86 percent markets are *developing*. Although it will take decades for these markets to become developed, the certainty is that they will continue to change rapidly. In a year, or even a matter of months, these markets can shift. Look at the rapid emergence of South Korea over the past decade or the growth of India and China. Consumers become upscale. The precise trajectory this development will take will depend on factors such as government regulations, traditional business practices and culture, and companies' actions. Rising incomes and improved economic conditions will change consumer habits and society itself, creating predictable shifts, such as the increasing empowerment of women, as these markets mature. These markets will present new challenges and opportunities at each stage of their development.

> Opportunity: By understanding the complex path to development, companies can evolve their businesses to meet the changing needs of the developing world. They can experiment with new products and business models in one country and export the successes to another, or even to the developed world. Companies also can import successful ideas from the developed world as the 86 percent markets mature. How can you develop your business with the market?

Because of these distinctive characteristics of the 86 percent market, companies often need to employ market solutions that are quite different from those of the developed world, as summarized in Table 1-1. Each characteristic creates market opportunities with the right strategies, as we will examine in more detail in the following chapters.

TABLE 1-1   Unique Characteristics Create Market Opportunities

Market Characteristic	Strategy for Realizing Market Opportunities
Markets, culture, and environments are demanding.	Don't build a car when you need a bullock cart.
There are high rates of emigration to the developed world.	Aim for the "ricochet economy."
Markets are fragmented.	Connect brands to the market.
Populations are youthful and growing.	Think young.
There is limited income and space.	Grow big by thinking small.
Infrastructure is weak.	Bring your own infrastructure.
Technology is underdeveloped.	Look for the leapfrog.
Distribution channels are weak.	Take the market to the people.
Markets are changing rapidly.	Develop with the market.

Finding Solutions

Success in the 86 percent markets often means challenging conventional wisdom. In banking, for example, Grameen Bank, founded by Professor Muhammad Yunus, offered microloans to village businesses that wouldn't have received a second glance from mainstream banks. Grameen began in one village in Bangladesh in 1976 and now has more than 3 million borrowers and a staff of more than 11,000 in more than 43,000 villages. With a loan recovery rate greater than 99 percent, Grameen Bank has been profitable every year since 1992, financing its loans almost entirely from its own funds and the savings of depositors. Grameen has become a trusted brand name that has led to other related businesses. According to UN estimates, somewhere between 70 million and 750 million microloans were offered by thousands of lenders worldwide in early 2005. The microlending model has been picked up by for-profit microlenders such as Basix in India, which provides financial services to rural borrowers in nearly 10,000 villages in India. Microlending has swept into the mainstream, along with a mind-set that allows companies to see the hidden opportunities in these markets. This shift in thinking is reflected in a 2004 advertisement for global investments by U.S.-based Franklin Templeton Investments that proclaims: "You see an ancient culture. We see modern homeowners." (See Figure 1-5.)

FIGURE 1-5 A Franklin Templeton advertisement recognizes that there are more opportunities in the 86 percent markets than meet the eye. (Courtesy of Franklin Templeton Investments. Copyright 2004–2005. Franklin Templeton Investments. All Rights Reserved.)

Millions of customers for financial services were invisible until someone created a business model to reach them. At the other end of the spectrum, companies are competing for private banking customers among a growing pool of affluent consumers in the developing world. These customers also only recently emerged or have been recognized. How many other potential customers are waiting out there for an organization to come in with the right solutions? Companies that have created strategies tailored for the 86 percent of the world's population in developing markets have found tremendous opportunities, but this requires rethinking products, branding, distribution, and many other market strategies.

Developing markets can present very difficult challenges, with poor sanitation; lack of water, food, and clothing; housing shortages; and lack of education. But in the midst of these challenges, tremendous opportunities exist, in both the segments of the market that already have comfortable incomes and the segments that are still aspiring to rise from poverty. Companies can work with nongovernmental organizations (NGOs), governments, and other organizations to address the pressing needs of these countries while building profitable businesses. In the following chapters, we'll explore in more detail the opportunities created by the unique characteristics of the 86 percent markets and some of the solutions for realizing them.

The 86 Percent Solution

- Examine each of the characteristics of the 86 percent market, and consider how you need to change your market strategies and products for these markets.

- Identify your current successful market strategies in developed markets that will not work in the markets. How do you need to transform these strategies?

- Assess the total market size for your product or service offerings in specific developing markets. Do you have rivals who can capitalize on these markets? What can you learn from their models?

- Look at the initiatives of NGOs, governments, and entrepreneurs in meeting the needs of specific developing markets. What can you learn from them? How can you work with them to develop business opportunities while meeting social objectives?

Notes

1 Kenichi Ohmae. "The $10,000 Club." *Across the Board*, October 1996, p. 13.

2 John Maynard Keynes. *The General Theory of Employment, Interest and Money* (1936).

3 General Electric 2004 Annual Report, February 11, 2005.

4 Dominic Wilson and Roopa Purushothaman. "Dreaming with BRICs: The Path to 2050." Goldman Sachs, Global Economics Paper No. 99, October 1, 2003.

5 Society of Indian Automobile Manufacturers, http://www.siamindia.com/General/production-trend.aspx.

6 Gabriel Kahn, Dan Bilefsky, and Christopher Lawton. "Burned Once, Brewers Return to China—with Pint-Size Goals." *The Wall Street Journal*, March 10, 2004, p. A1.

7 Peter Drucker. "Meeting of the Minds." *Across the Board* (*The Conference Board*), November-December 2000.

2

Don't Build a Car When You Need a Bullock Cart

Product design needs to reflect the challenges of the local environment and the demands of the local culture and religion. When you're looking for creative solutions to these needs, sometimes a bullock cart is better than an automobile.

The alarm goes off on Mahmoud's Ilkone i800 cell phone, with the muezzin's voice calling him to prayer. He pulls his Lexus sedan off the road at one of the mosques in Beirut, Lebanon. For when he is traveling, the phone has time-zone adjustments for thousands of cities and a built-in compass that shows him the direction to Mecca. He is a senior manager at a company involved in metal fabricating for the automobile industry. It has been a profitable business, which Mahmoud has helped build. The growing popularity of the annual Middle East International Auto Show in Dubai, which has swelled to more than 500 models from

Ikone 800

64 manufacturers, is a sign of the growth of the industry in the region. The show features high-end models from Mercedes, Jaguar, and Ferrari, as well as mid-range models from GM, Ford, Suzuki, and Peugeot. With a young population, the future opportunities in the domestic auto market are expected to continue to grow.

As he leaves the mosque, however, Mahmoud thinks about the challenges of political unrest and threatened sanctions against Iran, which have made the future of the business uncertain. Mahmoud and his colleagues are working hard to establish new markets in less-volatile regions in other parts of the developing world. But this means adapting to different sets of rules from the eccentric, but well-known, rules of markets closer to home. As he stops at a small shop and buys a Mecca Cola between meetings, he receives an instant message from his wife, Aghdas. She is on a break at work and wants to discuss a house she found on a real estate website. They have decided to purchase a bigger home, thanks to a new Sharia mortgage. As devout Muslims, they did not want to take a standard Western mortgage, but these new mortgages allow them to pursue their dream of owning a home without compromising their values.

The world has more than a billion Muslims, and almost all of them live in developing countries, along with diverse groups such as Hindus, Buddhists, Christians, and even atheists. How do you join modern technology with ancient culture and heritage? Are you designing products and services for this market? Most of the developing world population is in rural villages. Are you designing products and services that are relevant to the dirt roads of these markets? Do these customers need a car or a better bullock cart?

In a world of rutted, narrow village streets, the bullock cart may have an advantage over a performance sedan. This traditional large-wheeled cart drawn by lumbering beasts will not raise your status with the neighbors, nor will it break any speed records, but it will transport a substantial cargo from point A to point B. When Hindustan Motors, India's oldest car company, teamed up with an Australian partner to create a vehicle specifically designed for rural India, it didn't look to cars and trucks from the developed world for inspiration. Instead, the company created a vehicle designed to compete against the traditional bullock cart.

The resulting boxy Rural Transport Vehicle (RTV) is designed to move both people and goods (see Figure 2-1). It is slender enough to fit down narrow village streets, with a tight turning radius and good ground clearance. It is tough enough to traverse the uneven roads of India's countryside, with eight gears to go from creeping along rural roads to reaching high speeds on paved highways. It is a modern bullock cart. Recognizing the diverse demands on vehicles in rural villages, it has folding seats to haul two tons of cargo or carry as many as 20 people at a time. The RTV employs the most sophisticated technology available, including contemporary engineering and high emissions compliance equivalent to European standards.

FIGURE 2-1 Hindustan Motors—Rural Transport Vehicle (RTV). Which would you rather have on a muddy rural highway, a shiny luxury car or this RTV?

The design was based on insights from an extensive study of villages across India, and it is tailored to the specific needs of these markets. It is a low-maintenance vehicle for an area in which service is expensive and hard to find. It has good shock absorbers for ancient highways covered with potholes. It is versatile, making it useful as a people carrier, delivery van, troop carrier, school bus, and even ambulance. Like the minivan or SUV in the U.S., this RTV has defined its own category of vehicle. And like the SUV in the U.S. market, the RTV designed for the villages became a hit in urban markets, delivering schoolchildren and other passengers along the narrow streets of Delhi and other cities. The vehicle, offered in a natural-gas-powered version, also benefited from new environmental regulations. Although initial sales of the RTV failed to cover production costs, the natural-gas-powered RTV was relaunched and renamed the "Road-Trusted Vehicle" to coincide with restrictions on polluting diesel vehicles. It became a great success for Hindustan Motors. In fiscal 2001, the RTV was credited with turning around the company's sagging fortunes, with sales of more than 3,000 units generating revenue of more than 1 billion rupees (US$23 million). The company also began expanding sales in Bangladesh, Nepal, African nations, and other developing markets. By 2003–2004, nearly 60,000 multipurpose vehicles were sold in India, an increase of 14 percent over the previous year.

Hindustan Motors' RTV illustrates the value of looking closely at the market's true needs, appreciating its differences, and designing products to meet them. The RTV is certainly not the only solution to the diverse needs of developing markets. Many successful sedans, SUVs, and vehicles look much more like those of developed markets (although even these are usually tailored to local conditions in less visible ways).

Designing for Six-Yard Saris

Each segment needs its own "bullock cart" strategy, and solutions for different segments look very different. While Hindustan Motors focused on the rural segment in developing its bullock cart RTV, Ford developed the Ikon to capture the hearts and wallets of a growing middle-class market in India. Like many Western companies entering developing markets, Ford initially had tried to import cars from the developed world (starting with the Model A in 1907). After leaving the market in 1954, Ford returned in 1995 when the government approved a joint venture with Mahindra & Mahindra Ltd. (M&M) to sell the Ford Escort, targeting the entry-level, mid-size market that Maruti Suzuki's Esteem had dominated for nine years. Although the Escort had been a huge success in Europe, it received a lukewarm reception from Indian consumers. It was not designed for them.

In November 1999, Ford set out to create the first car built specifically for India by a multinational company. Engineers road-tested the car across the toughest Indian conditions, from the choking city traffic of Delhi, to the monsoon-flooded roads of Chennai, to the humidity of Kerala, to the rough roads of the Madhya Pradesh, and up the steep hills of Ooty. Engineers drove it from the snowy conditions of Simla to the scorching deserts of Jaisalmer and raced at high speeds along the empty stretches of road in Rajasthan. During these tests, sophisticated evaluation systems measured the temperatures of the coolant, brakes, fuel, and interior.

The results of Ford's tests led to changes in the car's design, including details such as a more robust horn, which is used far more in India. Ford added a new hydraulically operated clutch system and upgraded clutch lining to accommodate the Indian driving style of starting in second gear. The company also improved body sealing to address the high level of dust and water. Ford created a tight turning radius for sharp turns on narrow roads, increased front-end height for extra clearance, and added stiffness in the body structure to minimize road shocks. The Ikon built on Ford's engineering and reputation for low maintenance requirements, with service intervals of 15,000 km, long-life spark plugs, maintenance-free camshaft drive and valve clearances, a low-maintenance accessory drive belt system, and a sealed-for-life transaxle.

Ford recognized that a large number of cars, even at this price range, are chauffer-driven or had children and parents sitting in the backseat. Therefore, Ford increased the comfort of the backseat and added rear air conditioning. (Other companies learned the hard way about the importance of backseat design. When General Motors launched the Opel Astra in India in the 1990s, for example, its weak backseat air conditioning created many dissatisfied customers.) The car also was designed with high door apertures and wide door openings to allow women wearing six-yard-long saris to easily enter and exit.[1]

While the car was designed to meet the practical demands of Indian driving conditions, Ford also paid attention to the motivation of customers, with positioning around the idea of "josh" (full of life). Ford offered innovative financing mechanisms to put monthly payments for the Ikon within the reach of a broader segment of the Indian population. It also offered 24-hour emergency support, extended service hours, and a website for managing loyalty programs and building long-term relationships with customers. Furthermore, Ford offered professional service, including rigorously scheduled appointments, a system for a thorough vehicle check, and work orders that were reviewed with customers before repairs were made.

Only 6,000 Escorts were sold in the two years prior to the Ikon's launch. Ford sold five times as many Ikons (30,000) between February 2001 and 2004, despite tough competition. Ford's Ikon rode past the Esteem to become the leader in this segment, with 22 percent market share. Building on its successes, Ford India launched new models of the Ikon and a moderately priced SUV for the Indian market. By driving through the mountains and deserts of the local terrain, Ford was able to create a "bullock cart" solution for this middle-class segment. It faces tough competition from innovative companies creating next-generation "bullock carts," including Tata Motors (working on a US$2,000 car), partnerships such as Maruti/Suzuki and GM/Daewoo, and Romanian carmaker Dacia (recently acquired by Renault).

Another "bullock cart" solution at the low end of the market is the "Basic Utility Vehicle" (BUV). It's a roofless four-wheel vehicle designed by the U.S.-based nonprofit Institute for Affordable Transportation (see Figure 2-2). This vehicle is targeted toward microbusiness owners with incomes of less than $4,000 per year in developing markets with moderate weather. It has no windshield or doors. Its top speed is 20 mph, and it achieves fuel efficiency of 60 miles per gallon with a diesel or gas engine. It's also easy to maintain. The BUV arrives in a kit costing as little as $900. It's made primarily of simple materials and scrap auto parts, which can be shipped easily in ocean containers. The BUV is also well-suited for local manufacture, with low investment, simple equipment, and low skill requirements.

FIGURE 2-2   Without a roof or windshield, the Basic Utility Vehicle is designed for easy, low-cost maintenance to serve microentrepreneurs in developing countries with temperate climates. (Source: Institute for Affordable Transportation)

Back to Basics

Companies obviously have to redesign products and services to meet the demands of any global market. However, because the conditions of developing markets—from income to infrastructure to culture—are so different from developed markets, the solutions may not look anything like those created for developed markets. This requires not only adapting current products but sometimes creating a totally different product. Don't assume that you can just import the products and strategies of the developed world. Some need to be adapted, and others need to be redesigned from the ground up to meet local conditions. In addition to poor roads and narrow streets, factors such as culture, religion, and traditions demand different solutions, as we will explore in this chapter.

Strategy #1: Recognize That Low Price Doesn't Mean Low Quality

The developing world demands high quality at a lower price, so companies have to create solutions that deliver higher performance in some ways at a lower cost. For example, architect Simone Swan and adobe builder Maria Jesus Jiminez created a 550-square-foot adobe home as a demonstration model in Ojinaga, Mexico that cost just US$5,000. It was based on Middle Eastern architecture adapted to Mexican style, and the thick adobe walls made it less expensive to heat and cool. This solution allowed for cheaper construction cost *and* lower operating costs compared with typical concrete-and-lumber construction, which requires expensive heating and cooling systems. These houses could be constructed by teams of 20 families without using paid contractors.

Grameen Bank created a housing program in Bangladesh that provided would-be homeowners with loans of just $350, four concrete columns, a prefabricated concrete slab, 26 corrugated iron roofing sheets, and a design for a flood-resistant home. In the first five years of the program, some 44,500 homes were built, and 98 percent of participants paid back the loans.

Similarly, companies can lower maintenance and lifetime cost of ownership through product innovations. If companies design a car that is less likely to need repairs, or if they build insurance into the product, it may have a much higher value in these markets. The incorporation of dent-resistant panels in automobiles can help avoid bodywork down the road. Such innovations may increase the purchase price initially (although not always) but reduce the cost of ownership down the road. Instead of looking at only the purchase price, look at the lifetime cost of ownership to find ways to lower maintenance costs without significantly increasing the purchase price.

Strategy #2: Create or Import Innovative Solutions

As mentioned, companies such as Hindustan Motors and Ford have found opportunities by creating solutions tailored to local market conditions. Companies also can look for applications of innovative product designs to meet the challenges of the developing world. For example, several "best products" of 2004, as recognized by *BusinessWeek* and *Fortune*, might have applications in the developing world. Oral-B launched Brush-Ups in the U.S. market, disposable fingertip toothbrushes with toothpaste already on them. They are designed for busy people who want to clean their teeth after a meal without carting around a toothbrush and toothpaste. Because they are dry, they require no water or rinsing. Could they be brought to markets with scarce water supplies? Or a FLO bicycle, which folds into a suitcase as carry-on luggage for the developed world, could have potential as a space-saving bike for the small apartments of the developing world (if the $2,000 price tag could be reduced).

While most pharmaceutical companies are developing solutions for the U.S. and other developed markets, which are seen as primary markets that can support the expense of research and development, other companies are focusing on creating solutions for the developing world. Merck's well-known river blindness treatment, AIDS treatments developed by Indian pharmaceutical firm Cipla and other companies, and AstraZeneca's research center in Bangalore, focusing on tuberculosis, are concentrating attention on the challenges of the developing world. Although these markets used to be considered too poor to support drug development, a combination of support from foundations such as the Bill & Melinda Gates Foundation and public initiatives is creating more viable markets. Major pharmaceutical firms such as Dr. Reddy's Laboratories, founded by Dr. Anji Reddy, and Ranbaxy have emerged from the developing world.

Strategy #3: Cater to Customers Who Don't Know How to Be Customers

Consumers in many emerging markets have a history of living in environments in which supply could not meet demand. In countries such as Brazil, Iran, Romania, and Hungary, customers often had to wait for years to receive a telephone line. No fighting occurred among carriers with different pricing plans, as in developed markets. Some people would celebrate when they received a telephone line, and others would sell their number on the black market at a much higher price. Demand greater than supply meant that there was little need for high-quality service or guarantees to keep customers. In contrast, when supply is greater than demand, as in the developed world, the customer is king. It can take customers a while to get used to wearing this new crown. They have little experience with consumerism, so their consumer behavior can be unpredictable.

For example, in most developed markets, Amway uses a no-questions-asked money-back guarantee to signal product quality. If customers are not completely satisfied with the company's products, they can return the bottles for a full refund or replacement, even if they are empty. This guarantee showed that the company stood behind its products unconditionally. When Amway offered the same guarantee in China in 1997, it ran into trouble. Customers began returning empty bottles for refunds after using the product. A barbershop found that it could use Amway shampoo for free, returning every empty bottle for a full refund. Then enterprising third parties began repackaging the soap and returning the empty bottles right away. Unemployed Shanghai residents paid $84 for an initial set of products as an Amway distributor and *never ran out*. Others just scrounged empty bottles from trashcans and turned them in for refunds. One enterprising collector received nearly $10,000 for sacks full of old bottles.

When refunds mounted to $100,000 per day, Amway realized something was fundamentally wrong. The company changed its policy in China, implementing a more rigorous process for screening distributors and others who had made a business of returning empties. Did this settle the matter? Not at all. This move provoked howls of protest from distributors and bottle collectors. Hundreds of angry distributors marched into company offices to complain. They felt they were entitled to the refunds. Amway had offered the same guarantee in developed countries, where returns were reported at less than 2 percent. The company was understandably surprised by the Chinese reaction.

Similarly, Domino's Pizza took off rapidly in one Latin American country, but for the wrong reasons. Customers saw its 30-minute delivery guarantee as a challenge. They did their best to present the most complex and confusing addresses to slow the driver and receive a free pizza. It was not a service guarantee; it was a competition.

What these companies learned is that customers in developing markets lack an understanding of consumerism. *They don't know how to be customers*. They don't have the experience with concepts such as lifetime guarantees that are taken for granted as the starting point in developed markets. This needs to be understood in designing product and service offerings. In China, Amway probably didn't need a money-back guarantee to sell its product. Customers didn't expect this. Since the company's goal was to signal high product quality, there may have been other ways to send the same message that would have been less risky than offering the guarantee. Amway might have used endorsements or independent tests to certify quality.

Customer behavior also affects the overall experience of other customers. For example, JetAirways, founded by Naresh Goyal, offers modern and professional air service within India, with ambitions to become a global airline. However, when travelers don't want to stand in line at the ticket counter, or when they act rudely during the flight (see the sidebar), they erode the flight experience for other passengers. Customers in a fast-food restaurant such as McDonald's who do not know how to bus their own trays detract from the experience for other customers. Employees who have not been raised in a customer culture also will face an uphill battle in providing effective customer service. How can companies measure and improve service quality if it can be affected by the lack of consumerism by other customers and employees?

Unfriendly Skies

China has created one of world's largest passenger airline fleets and state-of-the-art airports, transporting 80 million passengers in 2004. But this rapid growth has a downside. On any given flight are many passengers who have never flown before. These passengers don't know how to be customers. Flight attendants are forced to deal with first-time flyers who don't know to buckle their seatbelts, who are rude, or even who try to open the emergency door in mid-flight. A flight delay might lead to customers shouting for dinner or demanding to leave the plane. This has resulted in a high level of burnout for flight attendants, despite relatively attractive salaries.

The dark side of a rapidly expanding middle class in developing countries is that many customers, such as inexperienced air travelers, are entering consumer markets for the first time. This means that no matter how advanced the equipment and clear the skies, it is often a bumpy flight.

Companies need to be aware of the lack of consumer culture. They need to design offerings and educational programs to compensate. Governments have successfully used education to promote hygiene, health, and public safety (to the point that Singapore was referred to as a "fine city" for its enforcement of many public improvement initiatives). For example, when Shanghai authorities began enforcing traffic rules more rigorously, citizens were not ready to accept this, and it led to an increase in assaults on police officers. In August 2004, government officials created a market system to change this behavior, offering a reward for snapshots or videos of violators. This approach led to more than 5,000 fines within the first three months. They not only caught violators, but they also educated the public about the importance of following these rules. Companies might use similar strategies to reward and change consumer behavior. They also can work around the lack of a consumer culture. For example, some fast-food restaurants are hiring employees to bus trays instead of trying to train customers to do so. This also enhances the upscale image these companies have in developing markets.

This lack of customer culture can also be seen in the absence of critical restaurant and theater reviews. When *Time Out* launched its Beijing edition in May 2003—as well as issues in Mumbai, Moscow, and other developing markets—restaurant owners were shocked to face critical articles from anonymous reviewers for the first time. These restaurants were used to receiving favorable reviews in publications in which they advertised. There was no concept of this critical aspect of a consumer culture—publications in service of consumers— but the magazine is helping to change that. There may be opportunities to create other such channels to serve an increasingly empowered and informed set of consumers.

Strategy #4: Respect the Power of Religion and Culture

Religion and tradition have a deep impact on how products and services are received in developing nations. People might go to a priest to
have a new computer or automobile blessed. While religion and tradition have an impact on the progress of businesses in any country, these
forces tend to be deeper and stronger in developing markets, which
makes it more important to recognize and address them. For example,
the World Health Organization estimates that up to 80 percent of the
African population uses traditional medicine. This has a significant
impact not only on public health but also on opportunities for alternative medicines as well as pharmaceuticals. The diversity of religions
and cultures across developing countries can also be quite dramatic,
making it difficult for outsiders to understand.

Consider how the Muslim seal of approval that a product is *halal*
affected soap competition in Bangladesh. Unilever's Lux was the
dominant soap in Bangladesh until 1996, with a line of tallow-based
soaps sold under the Bengali slogan *"Shaundarjer shuchanay Lux"*
("Beauty begins with Lux"). At that point, a new entrant, Aromatic,
seized substantial market share based on a claim that its vegetable-
based soaps were superior to the animal-based soaps of Lux. In its
advertising, Aromatic claimed its vegetable-based product was *halal*,
making it more acceptable to Bangladesh's predominantly Muslim
population. By 1998, Aromatic had seized 31 percent of the market,
before competitors with similar products began eroding its share. The
halal campaign was very successful and unexpected. While it is not
clear whether the claims about Lux's not being *halal* were accurate, the
perception was enough to drive down the Lux brand to half its market
share in a rapidly expanding market. Lux later reformulated its products to use a vegetable base and regained its market leadership.
Aromatic ultimately lost ground as a variety of other *halal* rivals moved
in and price competition intensified, and its market share fell to just
7 percent. But the experience offered important lessons about the
power of religion and culture in emerging markets.

Other companies have also built powerful advantages by catering to culture and religion (see the sidebar). In Europe, the emergence of *halal* fried chicken has challenged KFC, riding on the wave of growth of large immigrant populations. McDonald's even offers *halal* Chicken McNuggets in the Detroit area, which has a growing Muslim population. Websites have emerged that offer travelers tips on where to find halal, kosher, Hindu vegetarian, or other foods from home around the world.

Islamic Banking: Owning Your Home "the Sharia Way"

Citibank, USB Warburg, HSBC, and other companies have set up Islamic banking arms to offer financing, mortgages, and even hedge funds tailored to the restrictions of Islam's Sharia Law. Guidance Financial Group advertised home financing in 2004 with the headline "Achieve Peace of Mind This Ramadan by Owning Your Home the Sharia Way." The structure of these accounts and financial instruments had to be rethought to address religious restrictions on earning interest (usury) and requirements to make contributions to the poor, as well as prohibitions on monopolies and hoarding. Instead of fixed-interest accounts, Islamic banking offers savers more risky, open-ended mutual funds using partnerships and profit sharing.

For example, Citibank offers five Islamic banking products in Malaysia (home financing, unit trust, time deposit accounts, savings accounts, and checking accounts). Its home financing offering is fundamentally different from the mortgages in other parts of the world. The buyer finds the home of his dreams, the bank assesses the buyer's needs (length of financing and repayment terms), and then the bank purchases the house from the developer. The bank sells the house back to the buyer at a higher price, reflecting the selling price and the bank's profit margin. The buyer pays the selling price through fixed monthly installments over the agreed-on period. Thus, no interest is charged, but the bank still earns a profit. Similarly, checking and savings accounts are used for investments in businesses with upright values, and the bank distributes part of the profits as a reward to account holders. Islamic banking funds grew from 7.3 percent of Citibank's portfolio in 1997 to 12.6 percent in 2003. Citibank's parent, Citigroup, completed more than US$5 billion in Islamic banking transactions between 2000 and 2004.

The portfolio of Islamic banking services continues to expand, with insurance and hedge fund offerings. In October 2004, the Sharia Equity Opportunity Fund was launched as the first Islamic hedge fund. It took developers two and a half years to develop a fund compliant with the Sharia Law, which proscribes the risk and speculation inherent in most hedge funds.

Cell phone makers are also tailoring products to Islamic markets. Companies such as South Korea's LG Electronics and Dubai-based Ilkone Mobile Telecommunication are offering cell phones targeted toward the world's 1.4 billion Muslims. These phones feature the full text of the Holy Qur'an with English translations, programmed calls to prayer (with the voice of the Azan), prayer times and Qibla directions for more than 5,000 cities, and Hijri Calendar converters. South Korea's Hosan Corp. sells handheld devices with digital versions of the Qur'an in Arabic and English.

Strategy #5: Look at the Deeper Meaning of Products

Products may have a deeper meaning than their utilitarian purpose. In rural India, for example, clothes are washed using a bar of soap rather than powdered detergent. Housewives view the act of rubbing the bar of soap on the clothes as a labor of love. It helps remove stubborn stains and is an economical way of using a laundry product. When Hindustan Lever introduced its laundry detergent in India in early 1988, it became the dominant brand. However, the company recognized that many customers still were using bars of soap for washing because hard work demonstrated their love for their families. In the eyes of Indian housewives, by using detergent, they were no longer looking after their loved ones as well, were not being economical, and were going against tradition and habit. How could soaking take away the dirt and grime without hard scrubbing? In this culture, a time-saving innovation actually had negative connotations.

Recognizing these hurdles to the adoption of powdered soaps, Hindustan Lever developed a detergent bar that offered all the benefits of a laundry soap in a traditional bar form, with the added benefit of superior performance in hard water. The company's Rin Bar gained popularity across India because of its fit with the washing traditions of the Indian market. Dual usage of bars and powders is unique to India, and Hindustan Lever has transformed the laundry soap market into a detergent bar market.

By recognizing the deeper meaning of cleaning clothes to Indian housewives, Hindustan Lever's detergent bar was a product that met the need for clean clothing as well as the demands of tradition and culture. It allowed mothers in the developing world to show their love for their families while achieving better results in laundering their clothes.

Many companies engage in surface tailoring of their products to developing markets without addressing these deeper elements of culture and religion. For example, Mattel achieved better success with its Barbie doll after replacing its blonde-haired, blue-eyed U.S. version with dolls tailored to 45 different nationalities in 150 countries around the world. The "multiethnic" Bratz dolls produced by MGA Entertainment appealed to an even broader and more diverse group of customers around the world, selling millions of dolls and significantly eroding Barbie's market share. The Little Farah Talking Doll takes this tailoring even further. This 12-inch doll that retails for US$19.95 not only wears Islamic dress but also recites 11 Islamic phrases in Arabic or English, such as *"Insh-Allah"* ("If Allah wills") and *"SubhanAllah"* ("Glory be to Allah"). On a related website, Little Farah's Corner (www.toytutors.com/products/farah/aboutme.asp), children can learn more about the doll's family and interests, including

basketball players Tarik Abdul-Wahad of the Dallas Mavericks and
Hakeem Olajuwon of the Houston Rockets. "They are excellent basketball players and also humble and devout Muslims," the site notes.
This doll is not just a toy but a means for Islamic parents to teach their
children their language and values and to convey aspirations.

Strategy #6: Market to the Memsahib

In taking products to developing markets, the housewife (*memsahib*
in India and *ama de casa* in Mexico) can play a central role as a hub
for introduction. A wealthy housewife in India or Mexico may set
the trends for maids and other employees in her household, a fact
that is often missed if companies focus on the end purchaser. Many
Indian households, for example, have part-time workers (such as
housekeeper, maid, cook, driver, or handyman) who regularly speak
with the housewife. She advises them on all kinds of problems and
on purchases as diverse as cough medicine and detergents to appliances and motor vehicles. By default, she is the decision maker for
as many as six families. But how many companies target her as the
most important point of influence for products designed for six families? If she herself uses these products, think for a moment about
the multiplier effect on sales. She also plays a much more active role
in the lives of her household staff than might be the case in developed countries. For example, it is not uncommon for her to make
sure a household servant's children attend school and to pay for
their schooling. She also might supply members of her household
with cell phones and other technology to help them keep in touch
with her.

Although the housewife herself may not be interested in buy-
one-get-one-free offers or credit card awards, she might give these
to her household staff. Very few companies pitch offerings in a way
that recognizes these relationships. But companies could offer the
housewife credit cards that provide rewards tailored to the needs of

the household workers. Instead of family plans for cell phones, companies might offer household plans that facilitate service for household employees with products that are designed, for example, to limit personal use.

Tradition and community can also be used to facilitate the adoption of innovations within developing countries. For example, the development of a market for gas fuel for cooking has used traditions of community cooking to introduce this new product to rural villages in India. Women in rural India traditionally have relied on cattle dung for cooking fuel, so propane gas distributor HPCL faced a challenge in converting rural consumers to gas. They used the tradition of community kitchens (*Sanjha chulha*) in rural villages, where women carry their kneaded dough to a centralized clay oven (*tandoor*) to bake their bread. By introducing propane to these central ovens, the company helped spread the adoption across the villages.

Traditions can help facilitate product acceptance, but they also can slow the introduction of new products. Companies need patience in introducing new products and services that require changes in habits. During the early 1900s, filtered oil and ghee (clarified butter) were the primary cooking media in India. Ghee with its buttery flavor was preferred, but when milk prices shot up in the 1920s, ghee prices also increased. It was then that Hindustan Lever in India introduced a breakthrough innovation, Dalda Vanaspati. This product not only had the rich aroma and flavor of ghee, but it also appeared the same, at a much lower cost because it was actually made of vegetable oil. Given the demand for ghee and the price advantage of Dalda, it would have seemed to be a fairly easy proposition to market the new product. Ghee, however, enjoyed a special equity from its long tradition in the country and importance in religious traditions, where offering an "imitation" product is frowned on.

Dalda eventually became a very popular product, but it took about 10 years. Hindustan Lever used a campaign of marketing demonstrations around the country, press advertisements, and door-to-door selling. Once it was accepted, it grew rapidly. In fact, it was such a huge hit that supplies became limited and customers lined up to buy Dalda at stores. The product was referred to as "black gold," and a black market developed. The high demand brought rival brands to the market. The government even stepped in to institute price controls and ensure supply. Dalda became the household name for this product that is now firmly a part of Indian culture. However, as the progress of Dalda Vanaspati shows, if tradition and culture can be harnessed and even transformed over time, this can create powerful opportunities for building markets.

Riding the Bullock Cart

Developing markets often differ in fundamental ways from developed markets, and the product and service solutions for these markets need to reflect these differences. Companies that want to realize the 86 percent opportunity need to first recognize the impact of these differences in environment, culture, religion, and customer experience.

Sometimes the resulting solutions need to be more like bullock carts than traditional automobiles. Quality needs to be high, but it might be defined differently. Offerings may need to be changed in significant ways to reflect local culture and religion. The way to a customer may be through the *memsahib*'s household. Sometimes solutions require merging the old and the new, the modern and the traditional. By understanding the differences, companies can build "bullock carts" that they can ride to profits and growth by meeting the market's true needs.

The 86 Percent Solution

- Consider how you need to tailor a specific product to reflect local conditions and challenges in a specific local market (such as people living in the Andes or in Shanghai).

- Identify the specific segments that will find your product or service offering attractive today, and look for ways to create other offerings for other segments (poor/rural, middle-class, luxury). Are you offering cars to customers who need bullock carts?

- Develop different strategies for a country with US$2,000 per capita GNP, one with US$5,000 GNP, and one with US$10,000 GNP. How do your strategies need to change?

- Look for ways to increase durability and reduce lifetime cost of ownership.

- Develop strategies for dealing with first-time consumers who don't know how to be customers. How do you need to change your offerings? What education can you offer?

- Examine how your products and services need to be tailored to local religion and traditions. How can you make your products more attractive to the more than 1 billion Muslim consumers? What other segments are you overlooking?

- Explore the communities and social networks that are critical to your company. Look for ways to appeal to the *memsahib* (housewife). How can you tap into these networks to build acceptance of new products?

Notes

1 As an indication of the potential for rethinking car design for specific markets, a five-woman team of designers at Volvo created a concept car designed for women. At the touch of a key fob, its gullwing doors slide up, and the whole chassis rises a few inches to allow easy access, even for pregnant women. The team also created a redesigned headrest that can accommodate ponytails. Furthermore, the team developed an "Ergovision" system that scans the driver's body at the dealership and then preprograms seat and other settings into the key fob so that the car is custom-fit to the driver. Isn't it time this was done for women in developing countries?

3

AIM FOR THE RICOCHET ECONOMY

With high rates of immigration to the developed world, the 86 percent market is stretched across zigzagging global diasporas. To reach the developing world, companies sometimes need to "ricochet" off social networks of the developed world.

Juan immigrated with his wife and son from Mexico to San Antonio several years ago and now has a job as a construction worker that allows them to afford a small apartment. They obtained their first Bank of America credit card, and they just received their first car loan. He makes frequent calls back to his parents and other family outside Mexico City, using AT&T or a calling card he purchased at the local 7/11 to budget his time. (He is looking into a Voice-over-IP service, which might make a broadband subscription worthwhile.) He recently purchased two bags of cement from Cemex that his brother picked up in his home village. It is a good feeling to finally be able to pave the floors of his parents' home. He has ordered them furniture from Famsa, a Mexican store whose website claims to be "tu tienda sin fronteras" ("your borderless store"). He also sends money orders back home to his parents and to clubes de oriundos, or hometown associations, supporting public-works projects. He recently opened an account with Citibank that allows him to deposit money in the U.S. that his parents can access in Mexico. Juan's apartment has been a little crowded ever since his brother-in-law, Javier, came to the U.S. He is staying in their apartment while he establishes himself, but it is much easier than when Juan came to Texas. Javier has received a "matricula consular" ID card from the consul general so that he can set up a bank account and obtain a driver's license. Juan and his family are planning their first flight back to Mexico on Aero Mexicana. He takes gifts back home and also plans to return with packages from Mexico, contributing to the local economy coming and going. Although he is a long way from his Mexican village, his heart and wallet are still close to home.

Immigrants like Juan are creating a networked economy stretching between developed and developing markets. They are collectively sending billions of dollars back to their native countries and creating demand for services in their new homes. How can you tap into this booming "ricochet economy"?

By catering to Hispanic immigrants in California, the founders of La Curacao electronics and furniture stores in Los Angeles built a diverse set of businesses with more than $250 million in annual revenues in 2004. Using its own credit formula, the retailer offers credit cards to recent immigrants who have an average monthly income of $1,500. Many of them are not citizens, and for 8 of 10, this is their first credit card. These customers are not even on the radar screens of other companies. Salsa music plays in the background, the staff speaks Spanish (some 40 million U.S. immigrants don't speak English), and mariachi bands and other entertainers perform on a stage. This is all the more remarkable because the store was started by a pair of Israeli brothers who were once illegal immigrants themselves. They may not have spoken the same language, but they certainly understood the needs of the market.

La Curacao then took its business a step further. It recognized that many of these Hispanic customers had family and friends back in Mexico or in other areas with much more limited means. The retailer introduced a system that allowed U.S. customers to purchase products for delivery to relatives back home. It had harnessed the power of the "ricochet economy." This economy works across a set of relationships between immigrants in the developed world and their family and friends back in the developing world. The end user of the purchase may be in the developing world, but the payment comes from the developed world.

Although most markets are considered independently (the U.S. and Mexican markets, for example), there are actually many connections between them. Social and family networks zigzag across the world. Marketing messages, purchases, and funds move across these networks with little regard for national borders, ricocheting or bouncing from one market to the next. This means that, as in the case of La Curacao, a company can sell a product to a customer in Los Angeles that is delivered to a family member in Mexico City. A customer in New York City can deposit money in an account for a relative in Bangalore. Rich opportunities exist in this ricochet market, but it is just becoming visible to creative companies such as La Curacao because it crosses typical geographic boundaries.

Person-to-person global capital movements, coupled with the strong social ties that bind the immigrants to family and friends back home, have created many paths back and forth between the markets of the developed and developing worlds. Since most of these workers go abroad to find work, and many intend to send money back home, this flow of income and goods back to the developing world is to be expected. These financial flows are not along the broad superhighways of traditional banking systems but rather are on small winding pathways between husbands, wives, and children. Along these paths, almost invisible, flow billions of dollars and the information that fuels markets.

By recognizing how communications, products, and capital bounce back and forth—or ricochet—between the developed and developing world, companies may find that the most direct route to a customer often is not a straight line, but rather a bank shot between the developed and developing worlds, as shown in Figure 3-1.

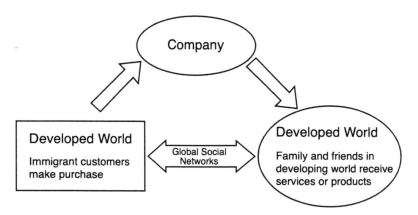

FIGURE 3-1   The ricochet economy.

The Ricochet Economy

Foreign immigrants working abroad sent home an estimated $93 billion in 2003, according to a World Bank study, nearly the equivalent of Singapore's entire gross national income (GNI). These remittances are the second-largest financial flow to developing countries, after foreign direct investment (at about $150 billion), as shown in Figure 3-2. The funds sent home by workers from abroad are more than double the size of net official financial flows and greater than capital market flows. Remittances have grown rapidly, jumping by 20 percent from 2001 to 2003, despite the many hurdles created by banking fees, exchange rates, and other obstacles.

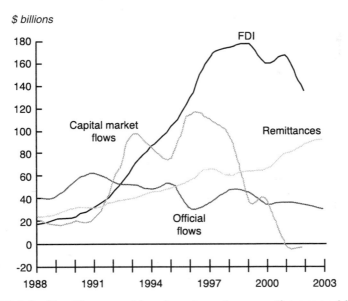

FIGURE 3-2   Remittances of immigrant workers are the second-largest source of resources flowing into developing countries, second only to foreign direct investment. (Source: World Bank)

The top source of workers' remittances is the U.S. The top destination for workers' funds is Latin America, a flow of capital that reached nearly $30 billion in 2003. Latinos in the U.S. had an estimated $652 billion in disposable income in 2003 and were expected to account for nearly 10 percent of all U.S. disposable income by 2008. Expatriate

Indians sent home more than $18 billion from different parts of the world in 2003, double the amount in 2000. With the collapse of the Soviet Union, some 400,000 immigrants have streamed into Portugal, accounting for about 10 percent of the workforce and about 20 percent of total bank deposits by the late 1990s. In Malaysia, 160,000 Indonesian maids were registered in 2003, and an additional 100,000 may have been working illegally, an immigrant workforce equivalent to more than a tenth of the country's 23 million population. By the 2000 census, more than 35 percent of New Yorkers were foreign-born.

The $93 billion was just the official tally for remittances; the actual figures are very likely much higher because such funds often move through the back channels of the informal economy (as discussed in Chapter 7, "Bring Your Own Infrastructure"). As one indication of the extent of these informal transfers, when restrictions after the 9/11 terrorist attacks made informal transfers harder, remittances to Pakistan through formal channels nearly tripled over the following two years. It is estimated that there are $10 billion in inbound remittances in China, with another $10 billion through underground services. And it is not just capital that is arriving off the books. There are high levels of illegal immigration. An estimated one in five marriages among immigrants in London could be sham marriages designed to circumvent immigration laws.

How significant are these remittances to developing economies? They represented more than 37 percent of the GDP of Tonga and a significant portion of the GDP of many other countries, as shown in Figure 3-3.[1] Mexican President Vicente Fox credited some $14 billion in remittances to Mexico from legal and illegal immigrants in the U.S. as a key factor in achieving a 16 percent decline in families living in poverty between 2000 and 2004, despite a stagnant economy. In addition to going directly to help families in developing countries, U.S. funds account for an estimated one-fifth of the capital invested in microenterprises in Mexico. One study in Mexico concluded that every dollar of remittances from workers abroad generated about three dollars in local spending power.

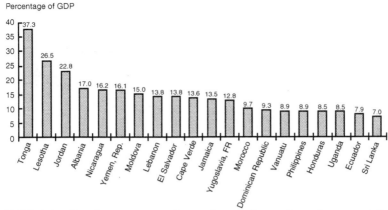

FIGURE 3-3 Remittances sent home by workers abroad account for a significant portion of the GDP in many developing countries. (Source: World Bank, 2004)

Catering to Immigrants

As policy makers have become more aware of the importance of capital flows from workers' remittances in country development, they are taking an interest in making these capital flows easier. Finance ministers from the Group of 7 (G7) industrial nations are pushing to integrate remittances into the formal financial sector, and the Inter-American Development Bank has persuaded financial services companies to cut the costs of transferring money in half. The World Bank has also recommended improvements to the financial infrastructure. These include reducing remittance costs, improving competition among money transfer agents, increasing access to banking services for migrant workers in source countries and households in recipient countries, and improving the investment climate by liberalizing exchange restrictions. Recognizing that three-quarters of Mexicans in the U.S. who remit funds have no bank accounts, the U.S. is loosening restrictions on identification. More than 100 U.S. banks now accept an identity card called the *matricula consular* and a taxpayer identification number to open bank accounts.

In the developing world, countries are also promoting these financial flows. Mexico, for example, has created a separate department focused on Mexican immigrants abroad, which is looking for ways to facilitate these transfers. India has established a similar ministry of nonresident Indian (NRI) affairs to manage contributions from overseas Indians to nongovernmental organizations (NGOs), maintain special economic zones for NRIs, and handle other related matters. India also has created an annual Pravasi Bharatiya Divas Day to strengthen bonds with Indians abroad. An annual award is presented to nonresident Indians, such as the posthumous recognition given in 2004 to Indian-born U.S. astronaut Kalpana Chawla, who was killed in the 2003 space shuttle *Columbia* accident.

Although crackdowns following 9/11 have made it harder for some immigrants to come to the U.S., immigration from the developing world to the developed world continues to be strong. In New York City, 6 in 10 babies born since the 1990s have at least one foreign-born parent, with the fastest-growing immigrant populations from Bangladesh, Mexico, and Pakistan. The Pew Hispanic Center estimated in 2002 that 12 percent of Mexico's population with higher education and 75 percent of Jamaica's was in the U.S. In 2002, the U.S. educated one-third of all students who studied abroad, and about half of the foreign students who earned their PhDs in the U.S. were still there five years later. (However, the development of domestic universities and business schools abroad has begun to cut into U.S. foreign applications.)

Taking Aim

While the World Bank and other organizations have begun to recognize the significance of expatriate remittances in the economies of developing nations, businesses are also starting to capitalize on the opportunities in the linkages of the ricochet economy, through the following market strategies.

Strategy #1: Develop the "Bank Shot"

As La Curacao discovered, the first strategy for the ricochet market is to create products and services that can be paid for by immigrants in the developed world for relatives or friends back home. Like a "bank shot" in the game of pool, the purchases bounce off the developed world to hit an end user targeted in the developing world. Here are some examples:

- Mexican-based cement giant Cemex has set up a system for Mexican immigrants in the U.S. to purchase cement for relatives in Mexico. The Mexican relatives can pick up the cement at a local store to use for building homes.

- Mexico's largest private mortgage company opened an office in New York City, facilitating the purchase of homes for relatives back in Mexico. Hipotecaria Nacional SA (Hipnal) offers loans to Mexicans working in the U.S. so that they can buy homes in Mexico. The company expects to open additional offices in other areas with high Mexican immigrant populations, including Arizona, Texas, and California.

- E-commerce sites naturally lend themselves to serving these immigrant populations abroad. Peruvian retailer E Wong, for example, advertises its online site to immigrants in California, New York, and other U.S. regions. These immigrants can purchase more than 50,000 products for relatives back in Peru. E Wong worked out an arrangement with Visa to facilitate payment for these overseas transactions. This allows fathers working abroad to make choices about products for their families and make sure the funds are used for necessities. Similarly, Argentineans in the U.S. purchase food and gifts for family back home through Discovirtual (http://www.discovirtual.com.ar). Famsa customers in Mexico can purchase appliances and furniture for relatives online at its "borderless store" (http://www.famsa.com.mx).

In addition, companies sell products in the developed world that are purchased and then carried to the developing world by immigrants or tourists on their trips back home. Retailers on Canal Street in Manhattan and Devon Avenue on the north side of Chicago, where streets are named after Third World leaders, sell 220-volt appliances and electronics that cannot be used in the U.S. but are designed for relatives and friends abroad. In addition to using the Internet, buyers also make trips to the developed world, such as a buyer from Peru who takes orders from his neighborhood during his shopping trips to Miami.

The world's borders are permeable, with nonresident populations connecting different markets in diverse parts of the world. Even if a market is formally closed by regulations and income limitations, as long as information is flowing, it is never really closed. The Internet only accelerates this process.

Strategy #2: Find Opportunities in the Flows

This flow of funds, people, and information across the ricochet economy creates business opportunities in supporting this movement:

- **Financial transfers**—Companies are creating systems to facilitate the efficient transfer of funds, such as workers' remittances from the developed to developing world. Retail giant Wal-Mart is offering its U.S. customers money transfers to Mexico for less than $10. Western Union has 225,000 outlets in more than 200 countries, including 21,000 in China, and 7/11 retail stores have set up a system for transferring funds in Mexico. ICICI Bank offers a free "Money2India" service that allows Indian workers in the U.S. or other parts of the world to send funds in 13 different currencies to 2,150 branches in 670 locations across India. These funds can be transferred electronically, by check, through a credit card, or by web-based wire transfers. Workers in Singapore, for example, can walk into remittance centers in Lucky Plaza or Little India and quickly transfer money back home. Traditional banks, with complex and expensive transfer procedures, have failed to capture much of the flow of remittances. According to one study, the four largest U.S. banks engaged in these transactions handle only about 3 percent of the 40 million remittance transactions to Mexico each year. Four of 10 remittances to Latin America are for $200 or less, and high bank fees, lack of access to banking services for migrant workers, and exchange restrictions mean that workers sometimes lose half the value of their funds in making small transfers.

- **Telecommunications**—Mexican phone-access receipts from the U.S. are the highest in the world, with 5.2 billion minutes in 2001, followed by Canada. India has been the fastest-growing destination, rising from 59 million minutes in 1991 to more than 1.4 billion minutes a decade later. Companies are recognizing opportunities in these communication flows. For example, Reliance Infocomm, Ltd., India's largest mobile service provider, has created an 11.9-cents-per-minute calling plan between the U.S. and India through both a prepaid plan and a pay-after-use plan, half the price of major U.S. competitors. Verizon, Nextel, and other companies have launched marketing campaigns for U.S. Hispanic customers, who spend an average of 10 percent more on cell phone calls and 6 percent more on monthly long-distance phone service than the average U.S. customer. Nextel has launched an international version of its walkie-talkie service that allows U.S. customers to directly connect to friends and family in Brazil, Argentina, Peru, and other Latin American countries.

- **Entrepreneurship**—Companies are also helping immigrant entrepreneurs from the developed world start businesses back home. For example, IndiaCo, a private-equity fund near Mumbai, supports many new businesses founded by foreign-born entrepreneurs in the U.S. These entrepreneurs, often with experience working at a U.S. high-tech firm, set up new businesses in software, biotech, nanotechnology, and other areas. Immigrants returning home recognize the value of setting up businesses at a fraction of the startup costs of a U.S. technology firm. They also appreciate the opportunity to give something back to their homelands. Venture funds in the U.S. are recognizing these opportunities, with San Francisco investment companies increasing their attention to and investments in Indian businesses. (Immigrants are also helping companies in the U.S. and other developed countries create strategies for the developing world.)

Companies that recognize the value of these flows might change their offerings to take advantage of them. Rather than a low volume of financial transactions at a high fee of $30 each, banks might gain a larger share of the $93 billion in transfers by foreign workers if they lowered or eliminated these fees, as ICICI Bank has done in India.

Strategy #3: Serve Immigrant Markets Abroad

Not all the income earned by foreign workers is sent back home. Some of it is spent in the developed world, but often for products and services related to the developing world. Foreign workers represent significant markets embedded within developed countries, and they are growing rapidly. The number of U.S. immigrants increased 57 percent between 1990 and 2000, at a time when the domestic population grew by just 9.3 percent. The largest immigrant populations in the U.S. were from Mexico, China, the Philippines, India, and Vietnam, as shown in Table 3-1.

TABLE 3-1   Origins of the Largest U.S. Immigrant Populations

Country of Birth	Number of People	Percentage of the Foreign-Born Population
Mexico	9.2 million	29.5%
China	1.5 million	4.9%
Philippines	1.4 million	4.4%
India	1.0 million	3.3%
Vietnam	1.0 million	3.2%

Source: Census 2000, American Demographics

This means that the U.S. has a population of foreign immigrants about the size of Canada—or all the citizens of Belgium, Portugal, and Greece combined. This is just in the U.S. It doesn't include the high immigrant populations in European countries and other parts of the developed world. These immigrants represent significant markets within developed countries, and companies are developing strategies such as Hispanic advertising and products to appeal to these markets. Targeting immigrants in the U.S. and other developed countries is facilitated by the concentration of immigrant populations. In the U.S., for example, immigrants are located in specific areas of the country, such as California, Texas, New York, and Florida.

These immigrants can often be served through products and brands imported from their home countries or created specifically for these segments. For example, multimedia sports information firm Sportsya offers Mexican soccer scores and other information through a text messaging service for U.S. Hispanic cell phone subscribers.

Frito-Lay brought four popular brands to the U.S. from its Mexican subsidiary Sabritas. Although the company had marketed Latin-flavored versions of Lay's and Doritos, the Mexican brand conveyed greater authenticity to Hispanic customers in the U.S. Although Frito-Lay initially restricted distribution of the Sabritas brands to small grocers in Mexican neighborhoods to avoid cannibalizing its flagship brands, the brands achieved about $100 million in sales in 2004. This response to the U.S. Hispanic market helped Frito-Lay achieve continued growth in a carb-cutting environment that hurt its traditional snacks.

The Patak Indian food company has become one of Britain's most successful brands, in large part by catering to immigrants with authentic Indian food. Founder L.G. Pathak arrived in the UK nearly penniless from Kenya in 1956. The company's products are now distributed in over 40 countries, including India.

As an indication of increased interest in Hispanic and other segments within the U.S. market, U.S. advertisers spent $3 billion on print and television advertisements aimed at Hispanic viewers in 2003 (although this represented just over 5 percent of their total ad budgets). These investments continue to rise, however, with SABMiller announcing a $100 million advertising agreement with Univision Communications, the largest Spanish-language broadcaster in the U.S. The *Miami Herald* launched a Spanish-language edition in 1987 to serve the region's growing Spanish-speaking population. Publisher Rumbo started a new chain of four Spanish-language newspapers in Texas in 2005.

Immigrants also create opportunities for the development of other services, such as language education. A dual-language public school near New York's Chinatown, for example, teaches students in both English and Mandarin. The children, 80 percent of whom are of Chinese descent, are learning Chinese characters from kindergarten. Although most U.S. students begin learning a foreign language in high school, foreign-language education in U.S. elementary schools experienced double-digit growth in the 1980s and 1990s. Some businesses serve immigrants abroad in arranging marriage ceremonies, adoption, entertainment, and other services. Immigrants join and support local temples, mosques, and other religious institutions. Companies are also creating diverse services to cater to the needs of these immigrants, including television targeted toward American Muslim and Hispanic audiences, and health-care centers that respect Muslim traditions.

Financial services companies that have been successful in Mexico are moving into the U.S. Hispanic market, and U.S. companies are moving into Mexico. Spain's second-largest bank, Banco Bilbao Vizcaya Argentaria, bought assets in Mexico and then moved north to acquire Texas-based Laredo National Bancshares to target the fast-growing U.S. Hispanic market. The move followed Citigroup's 2001 acquisition of Grupo Financiero Banamex SA, Mexico's second-largest bank, and Bank of America Corp.'s acquisition of 25 percent of the Mexican Unit of Santander Central Hispano SA.

Large immigrant populations also present opportunities to sell translation products. For example, CommuniCard has created a set of pocket communications cards for police and workers in various industries. These allow English speakers to communicate with multi-cultural people through the use of pictures.

Strategy #4: Welcome Travelers Back Home

In addition to the direct income from travel by immigrants returning home, other services are targeted toward this group. For example, many expatriates return home for a wedding, so there is an active market for traditional wedding services. New or restructured airlines such as no-frills AirAsia, JetAirways in India, and Aero Mexicana in Mexico have developed services catering in large part to immigrants returning home from abroad as well as the rising middle class within developing markets. International carriers have also joined with these local airlines through partnerships such as Star Alliance and OneWorld, as well as "check-in partnerships," to offer seamless service to returning immigrants and others traveling between developed and developing nations. These are sophisticated services with high standards of service and competitive pricing designed for travelers from the developed world.

Some retail shops in major cities are tailored to these returning immigrants, where shopkeepers speak English and accept credit cards. And more unusual cultural connections exist across borders.

For example, more than 20 percent of all Taiwanese men marry someone from the mainland, creating a thriving business in cross-strait matchmaking.

Strategy #5: Span the Network

In addition to products and services tailored to immigrants abroad, opportunities exist to create products that span these global networks or draw them closer together. Movies and other artistic offerings are a prime example of the opportunities for global success created by tapping into networks of immigrants abroad. For example, the hit Bollywood musical *Main Hoon Na* grossed $2.5 million in North America and the United Kingdom in just 10 days after its release in 2004. On its opening weekend, it was the 15th highest grossing film in North America and the seventh ranked film in the United Kingdom. Bollywood love story *Veer-Zaara* recorded the highest-ever opening of a Hindi film in Britain, taking fourth position when it opened in November 2004. The December 2004 release of *Swades* created a stir among immigrants that has been called the "Swades effect," as Indian immigrants have rushed to emulate the film hero's return to his native village.

Online communities can also span the network between home and immigrants abroad. The online community Sulekha.com has created a successful business by tying together the diffused global networks of Indians around the world. The website, the largest Indian online community, reaches hundreds of thousands of Indians from more than 100 countries. Sulekha grew rapidly after its founding in 1998, posting more than 100 percent growth per quarter without advertising. Sulekha lets participants share insights and opinions, view news and columns, sign petitions, book travel, post classified ads, seek a partner, or find out about concerts, movies, and other events. Sulekha provides city portals with specific activities of interest in 60 cities around the world. Almost all of its 3 million pages of online content have been contributed by members. Some of the site's content has been gathered into a book, *Sulekha Select*. Sulekha has been successful by weaving together the Indian global community.

The Internet creates many other opportunities to share information, transfer digital photos, and complete other transactions that span national borders. The global Chinese community has sites such as www.sina.com, www.sohu.com, www.china.com, and www.mitbbs.com. Mitbbs.com, catering to overseas Chinese in the U.S., has more than 20,000 users registered for an online dating service for $14.95. Sites such as www.mezun.com and www.turkserve.com link the Turkish community around the world.

Advertisers on these sites also span diverse markets. For example, an advertisement for LG air conditioners on the Sulekha home page takes viewers to a page that lists prices in both Indian rupees and U.S. dollars. The Chinese Sina.com site offers Pingo calling cards, with "free calls to China, Taiwan, Hong Kong, and more." Online greeting-card companies are also discovering opportunities to span the network, with cards tailored to Muslims, Hindus, or other groups (see Figure 3-4).

FIGURE 3-4   Online greeting cards, such as this one from Sulekha celebrating Diwali, a major Hindu festival, allow immigrants to keep in touch with traditions and communicate with friends and family around the globe. (Source: Sulekha.com)

More Bounce

The global social networks of the ricochet economy are likely to be more important as global international immigration continues. The U.S. Census Bureau projects that by 2050 nearly a quarter of the U.S. population will be Hispanic.[2] While many of these people will be U.S.-born, even successive generations will often have deep ties to their native countries and perhaps a greater economic capacity to act on these social connections. Improvements in technology, such as the continued spread of broadband, will also facilitate the interactions across these extended family and social networks.

Further shifts in regulations that facilitate financial transfers and government agencies designed to cultivate connections with nonresident populations will encourage these flows across borders. The consumer flows of the ricochet economy create many business-to-business opportunities—from outsourcing to global financial systems (although these are outside the scope of this book)—which help facilitate the growth of the ricochet economy. These changes create new opportunities for companies that can recognize the invisible pathways of these social networks to create ricochet market strategies or facilitate flows of people and capital. Instead of thinking about these markets and individual consumers in isolation, consider the connections. As consumers, these immigrants don't see a sharp separation between the developing and developed worlds. Look for ways to use these connections to build strategies that transcend income boundaries or nations' borders to take full advantage of the opportunities this ricochet economy presents.

The 86 Percent Solution

- If you are marketing in the developed world, look for ways to reach immigrant populations there.

- Explore opportunities to use connections with developed-market immigrants to build businesses in developing markets.

- If you are selling in developing countries, consider how you can use your position to reach immigrants in developed countries.

- Look for opportunities to facilitate the flow of money, information, communication, and travel between the developed and developing worlds.

- Consider how you can use the Internet and other technologies to link the far-flung communities of the global diasporas.

Notes

1 *Global Development Finance: Striving for Stability in Development Finance*. The World Bank, 2004, Washington, DC. http://www.worldbank.org/prospects/gdf2004.

2 "U.S. Interim Projections by Age, Sex, Race, and Hispanic Origin." U.S. Census Bureau, 2004. http://www.census.gov/ipc/www/usinterimproj/.

4

CONNECT BRANDS
TO THE MARKET

Global brands often have been humbled by small, local rivals in fragmented, developing markets. Companies need to find the right balance of global and local brands, or reinterpret these brands, to connect with the market.

Hongli takes a bus downtown in Harbin, China. At the bus stop, she visits a hole-in-the-wall store and purchases a Qoo juice drink that she sips on the way to an automobile dealer. She pulls out her Bird cell phone to call her husband to make sure he is on his way. They had planned to meet to look at cars before heading back to their apartment that evening. Her husband, Jianmin, works in financial services at a multinational company. With her own work as a secretary for a local firm, they have the growing income to afford an increasingly comfortable lifestyle.

It is their first car. She is partial to a Wanxiang model, while her husband is attracted to the Volkswagen (VW). She likes the styling of the Wanxiang and also feels they should support Chinese companies. He points out that he and many of their friends work for foreign firms—and besides, he likes the European feel of the VW. It makes him feel more sophisticated and more a part of the broader world. This decision has been a point of contention for them, but she is sure they will work things out. Price and financing may be the deciding factors anyway.

After they have taken a look at the Wanxiang offerings, they head back home, where they curl up to watch MTV on their TCL flat-screen television after checking their e-mail on their IBM ThinkPad. (Hongli notes with satisfaction that although her husband convinced her to buy a U.S. product in this case, it has now become a Chinese brand after the acquisition of IBM's PC business by Lenovo.) They take a couple of bottles of Harbin beer out of their Haier refrigerator and watch an advertisement for yet another automobile. Hongli is surprised at how the world can be so different from the one in which she grew up and yet still seem surprisingly familiar.

Citizens of developing markets such as Hongli and Jianmin purchase a mix of global and local brands as they connect with traditions and the broader world. How can you create or acquire the right mix of brands to appeal to these local markets?

What is a local brand worth in developing markets? After winning a bidding war with rival SABMiller, Anheuser-Busch agreed to pay more than US$700 million in June 2004 to buy Harbin Brewery in China. The final bid was about 50 times the brewer's 2003 net profit.

Anheuser-Busch wasn't trying to gain access to Harbin's brewing skills. The American beer maker wanted the 104-year-old brand of Harbin, the fourth-largest brewer in the Chinese market. Harbin is particularly strong in the important markets of the northeastern part of China, where Anheuser-Busch had a relatively weak position.

When they raced into China in the 1990s, these major companies thought that powerful global brands such as Budweiser or Miller would give them a red carpet into emerging markets. They were wrong. A decade after their arrival, the global brands were suffering. Australian company Foster's Group lost an average of US$15 million per year on its joint venture in China during most of the 1990s before taking a US$126 million charge on its investment in two of its three breweries. England's Bass Brewers sold its Chinese plant and left the country in defeat in 2000. The market remained fragmented, with the top 25 brewing companies holding less than 50 percent of the market. The leading brewing company, a domestic firm, controlled only 12 percent of the market in 2002.

The survivors have capitalized on local branding and distribution. While Interbrew initially expected to pursue a national (or even regional) strategy, it is now succeeding better with a "patchwork" strategy of acquiring local brands. SABMiller's Chinese partner holds 30 local brands. In September 2004, Carlsberg Beer acquired a 34.5 percent stake in Wusu Brewery in northwest China following investments in leading breweries in Tibet and the provinces of Gansu and Yunnan. The moves were designed to shore up its position as the leading international brewer in western China, home to a population of 100 million.

When Theodore Levitt wrote his landmark treatise "The Globalization of Markets" in 1983, he framed two decades of debate about global products and brands.[1] Levitt's controversial proposition was that the convergence of technology and globalization would lead to greater standardization across world markets, consistently eroding or erasing differences in national or regional preferences. Yet two decades of experimentation with global products and brands have demonstrated the continued power and relevance of local brands. This is particularly true in developing markets, where global brands may have negative associations.

Among the top 25 brands identified by *BusinessWeek* and Interbrand in 2004 (see Table 4-1), Samsung from South Korea (at number 21) was the only one from a country that is anywhere close to an emerging market. Rising new brands such as Haier, LG, Lenovo, Tata, and TCL are waiting in the wings, but global brands today are from developed countries. These brands have paved the way to rapid market growth for multinational companies sailing along the super-highways of mass media, distribution networks, and global economic systems. But they may have begun to meet their limits in the complex, fragmented markets of the developing world. Are these brands still relevant to the 86 percent markets of the developing world? Can they be made relevant? Can these brands from the developed world connect to these emerging markets?

TABLE 4-1   Top 25 Global Brands in 2004

Rank	Brand	Country of Ownership
1	Coca-Cola	U.S.
2	Microsoft	U.S.
3	IBM	U.S.
4	GE	U.S.
5	Intel	U.S.
6	Disney	U.S.
7	McDonald's	U.S.
8	Nokia	Finland
9	Toyota	Japan
10	Marlboro	U.S.
11	Mercedes	Germany
12	Hewlett-Packard	U.S.
13	Citibank	U.S.

14	American Express	U.S.
15	Gillette	U.S.
16	Cisco	U.S.
17	BMW	Germany
18	Honda	Japan
19	Ford	U.S.
20	Sony	Japan
21	Samsung	South Korea
22	Pepsi	U.S.
23	Nescafé	Switzerland
24	Budweiser	U.S.
25	Dell	U.S.

Source: *BusinessWeek*/Interbrand, *BusinessWeek* August 2, 2004

Market-Stall Economies

There is no Chinese market. There is a market in Shanghai, or in a neighborhood in Shanghai. There is no Indian market. There is a market in Mumbai or Chennai, or in their local neighborhoods. Developing countries are a collection of fragmented local markets in a country that is gathered loosely under a single flag. China has more than 660 cities, yet a mere 71 million of its 1.3 billion people live in its largest four municipalities. Markets across China differ greatly. For example, the wealthy coastal city of Xiamen has a nominal GDP of more than $6,000, six times the level of the western city of Xining. Medium-sized cities such as Harbin and Quingdao have populations the size of Switzerland.

These smaller markets represent the majority of the population by a long shot. Even if China or India were carved into dozens of smaller "nations," each would be a formidable market in and of itself. In these fragmented markets, different cities and regions are gathered like the stalls of a town market, each with its independent owner, history, and practices, which are often inscrutable to an outsider.

These fragmented markets have opened the door to the growth of local brands. Mexico has Bimbo bread, Cemex cement, Dos Equis beer, and Big Cola. Peru has Kola Real, and Turkey has Kola Turk. In fact, while North American consumers ranked brands such as Apple, Target, Google, and Starbucks as their top brands, almost all the top Latin American brands identified by BrandChannel.com are local, as shown in Figure 4-1.

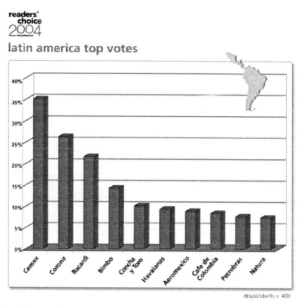

FIGURE 4-1   Many of the most respected brands in Latin America are local brands, although some of them have become significant global players. (Source: Brandchannel, 2004)

Of the top 500 brands in China based on advertising expenditures, 370 are local. The top 10 brands include not only Oil of Olay, Rejoice, Crest, and Head & Shoulders, but also Gai Zhong Gai, Arche, Aoqili, Sanjing Pharm, Softto, and Huangjindadang, as shown in Table 4-2. Some other brands that are not in the top 10 nationally have dominant positions in local markets. For example, Lafang, maker of hair care products (the 15th ranked brand), has virtually no share in the big cities but has built its market in small towns. Omo detergent, ranked 59th in the nation, has a 47 percent share in Shanghai but almost no penetration in rural areas.

TABLE 4-2 Many Domestic Brands Are Among the Top 10 Chinese Brands Based on Advertising Spending in 2003

Super Brand	Company	Category	Ranking	TV Advertising Spending
Oil of Olay	MNC	Toiletry	1	$1,265,357
Gai Zhong Gai	Local	Pharmaceutical	2	$1,247,019
Rejoice	MNC	Toiletry	3	$905,145
Arche	Local	Toiletry	4	$820,555
Aoqili	Local	Toiletry	5	$793,253
Crest	MNC	Toiletry	6	$671,991
Head & Shoulders	MNC	Toiletry	7	$627,886
Sanjing Pharm	Local	Pharmaceutical	8	$601,953
Softto	Local	Toiletry	9	$578,750
Huangjindadang	Local	Pharmaceutical	10	$568,162

In India, some of the world's biggest brands are fighting with home-grown heroes. Local brand Liberty became the top footwear company in India in late 2003, racing past megabrands such as Nike, Adidas, and Reebok. Liberty chose to strike from a lifestyle and fashion platform, associating itself with *India Fashion Week* and appealing to local tastes. Similarly, Killer jeans successfully took on the iconic Levi's brand. The top five Indian detergent brands control two-thirds of the market. The remaining one-third of the market for detergent in India is divided among more than 100 brands, mostly small local ones. More than 1,000 local competitors account for nearly 60 percent of packaged teas in India, and there are more than 100 brands of watches and 65 brands of televisions.

Brand Consciousness

Although every country has diverse segments, the extremes are greater and the fragmentation is deeper in the developing world. Long exposure to mass media in developed markets has provided decades of common ground for branding and positioning that doesn't exist in many developing markets. In these 86 percent markets, where media and consumer markets are just emerging, national and global brands also are still developing. While television, the Internet, and other media are spreading rapidly, changing the thinking and behavior of consumers is a relatively slow process.

Societies in the developing world, particularly in rural areas, are much more organized around local activity and interests. Yet these markets are still very conscious of brands. In the words of Adi Godrej, chairman of Godrej Group in India, which built a 10 billion rupee (US$228 million) agricultural business in rural markets, "It is a myth that rural consumers are not brand- and quality-conscious."[2]

This helps explain the initial failures of many multinational companies that entered China, India, and other developing markets with the brands, products, and strategies they use in the developed world. In cellular phones, Chinese companies such as TCL and Ningbo Bird surprisingly took the rural market from giants such Nokia and Motorola. Since most of them use outsourced components, they were competing not on technology but on the power of their local brands and dedicated retail networks. (The global cell phone companies, stinging from their early setbacks, have begun to learn how to play this game. They have been catching up rapidly by penetrating rural markets and tailoring products to local tastes.)

Strategies for Harnessing Local Brands

Given the complexities of branding for developing markets, how can companies best leverage their local and global brands to create opportunities? The following sections discuss some strategies.

Strategy #1: Make Your Global Brands Local

Companies such as MTV and HSBC have shown the power of creating a global, recognized brand that is tailored to individual markets. HSBC uses a decentralized management structure to ensure that local brands are responsive to their markets, a strategy reflected in its tagline of the "world's local bank." As an indication of the breadth of its reputation, in 2004 HSBC was named "Global Bank of the Year" by *The Banker* magazine, the "Most Admired Corporate Brand" by *Asiamoney* magazine, and the "World's Best Bank" by *Euromoney*. Five years after the launch of the global brand in the late 1990s, HSBC was already rated among the top 50 global brands.

The HSBC logo may look the same around the world, but this similarity masks the fact that it is seen as a local brand across more than 90 countries. "In most countries in which we operate, we are perceived to be a local brand," said Aman Mehta, former CEO, in an interview. "It has been a great success story in branding."[3]

For the strategy to be successful, HSBC has to have a superior product behind the brand, and operations really have to be local. "The main point in talking about a local bank is demonstrating to the customer that you are totally steeped in the local economy," Mehta said. "Even if a company talks about being local, it cannot wave a magic wand and become local. People have to be convinced of that over a very long period of time." HSBC's approach can be contrasted to Citibank, which created a more homogeneous culture and retained its identity as a U.S. bank.

Mehta said that this global brand was not established overnight. "In most of the geographies in which we operate, we have been working there for a very long time, often 100 to 150 years," he said. "We adopted a global brand strategy only when we were quite sure it would be more powerful than the local brands." When HSBC decided to use a global brand, intense debates resulted. One of the brands in the UK, Midland, had been in use since the 17th century. But the global brand with a local strategy prevailed. "This was not done lightly," he said.

In a speech in May 2004, HSBC Holding Group Chairman Sir John Bond noted that the same telecommunications and other technologies that have brought developing market outsourcing firms to the developed world are bringing global brands back home to the developing world. "The value of branding in a globalized world is enormous," he said, adding that "brand value will be more profitable than the value gained through offshoring service jobs."[4]

Recognizing the diverse languages of different parts of the world (see the following sidebar), MTV has localized its brand around the world, as discussed in more detail in Chapter 5, "Think Young." MTV India broadcasts primarily in Hindi, the dominant language of India, but it faces competitors broadcasting in Tamil, Telegu, and Punjabi. The company is considering launching or acquiring stations to reach listeners who don't speak Hindi, which is the primary tongue of only 30 percent of the population.

Microsoft created a platform for localizing the language of its Windows XP software. Through its Local Language Program, the company announced plans in March 2004 to develop Windows and Office software in 40 languages over the following year, building on versions in the Ethiopian language of Amharic and Ukrainian and other languages. The company announced plans in November 2004 to roll out software in the 14 official languages of India. The brand is still Microsoft, but the experience will be quite different for people in different regions. This tailoring of the brand to these local "markets within markets," making it relevant, will help Microsoft respond to the threat of open-source software such as Linux and expand the use of computers in these countries.

Although they are smaller than the total national market, these local markets are not small by any means. The Telegu-speaking area in Andhra Pradesh has a population of nearly 76 million people—a market about the size of Egypt. The tamil-speaking region of Tamil Nadu has more than 60 million people, about the population of the UK. As the market matures, MTV envisions that the Indian market might be treated like Europe, with different programs for different countries.

Plans for Disney's Hong Kong Disneyland theme park call for local foods and programs in two Chinese languages in addition to English. Disney also consulted a feng shui master in designing the park. After learning hard lessons with the initial missteps of Euro-Disney, Disney realized that it needed to find a delicate balance between preserving the attraction of a distinctly American brand and tailoring the experience to local tastes.

Do You Speak Hinglish?

Think English is the language to know for business? Maybe not for long. Consider that Mandarin Chinese has the largest number of speakers in the world—a billion, including second-language speakers. This is followed by English, with about half as many speakers, and then Spanish, Hindi, Arabic, Bengali, and Russian. If you want to work with the 86 percent world, you need to speak the languages of the 86 percent.

Even English is being affected by the rise of the developing world. Former P&G-India CEO Gurcharan Das has commented that if the 19th century was the age of British English and the 20th century the age of American English, the 21st century may well be the era of "Hinglish"—a combination of Hindi and English used by Indian speakers.

Strategy #2: Use Local Brands to Establish a Market Presence

Local brands can be a great asset, particularly in building a presence in a market. Anheuser-Busch recognized the value of local brands in acquiring Harbin. HSBC spent a century working with local brands in different countries before bringing them under the banner of its global brand.

Around the world, Coca-Cola has relied heavily on local brands to go where its flagship brand could not go. By 2004, the company owned more than 400 brands in 200 countries, earning about 70 percent of its income from outside the U.S. In Africa, the company sells 80 brands, with local beverages such as Sparletta, Hawai, and Splash. Coke has "taught the world to sing," but in different languages. In China, Coca-Cola offers water and tea products under its locally developed Tian Yu Di ("Heaven and Earth") brand, a successful carbonated juice-flavored drink called Smart, and a noncarbonated juice drink called Qoo, developed in Japan. It became the leading Asian juice drink in just two years. These global sales are increasingly important to Coca-Cola's future. While its 2003 sales growth was just 2 percent in the U.S., sales grew 16 percent in China, 22 percent in India, 14 percent in Thailand, and 10 percent in Mexico.

Groupe Danone SA, the French-based maker of cookies, yogurt, and mineral water, built a growing business in China by acquiring shares in local brands and by developing products for China under its own brand. By 2002, China had become its third-largest market, about equal to its sales in the U.S. The company reported growth in China of 10 percent over the prior year and profits higher than the global average. Its growth was driven by the acquisition of controlling stakes in Hangzhou Wahaha Group and Guangdong Robust Group, the leader in the nation's bottled water business.

eBay has entered India, China, and other parts of the world through local acquisitions. Its international strategy has been to look for "mini eBays," local companies that reflect the spirit of the original online auction company. This includes the acquisition of EachNet and Baidu in China, the acquisition of Baazee in India, and a majority stake in Internet Auction Co. in Korea. Despite eBay's strong brand recognition around the globe, these local brands represented particularly important portals into countries with growing Internet presence and limited retail reach.

The complexities for global companies in managing these local brands can be seen in the arrest of the head of eBay's Baazee unit in India in 2004 after a pornographic video clip was offered by a seller on the site. The manager, a U.S. citizen, faced up to five years in jail or a fine of 100,000 rupees (about $2,285) for violating India's Information Technology Act. Did the high profile of the parent brand contribute to the official attention?

Strategy #3: Grow Your Own Local Brands When Possible

As Anheuser-Busch found with Harbin, acquiring local brands can be an expensive strategy. While some local brands are based on century-old local dynasties, it is possible to create new local brands that pay close attention to market needs. In India, the detergent brand Nirma was created in the 1960s by Karsan Patel, a chemist who made detergents in his backyard and sold them on a bicycle. Today, the brand has 15 percent of the Indian detergent market. In response to the success of Nirma and other brands, Hindustan Lever established its own low-priced local brand, Wheel, in the 1980s. This new brand allowed the company to meet the needs of price-sensitive consumers without eroding the position of its established brands. Wheel, with a free-standing organization, became one of the dominant brands in the country.

Nirma built its brand by recognizing an opportunity in the consumer shift from low-cost laundry soap to more expensive washing powder in the 1970s. Hindustan Lever and other major global firms concentrated on the high-income segment that was already using washing powder while most Indians still used economical laundry soaps. The laundry soap market was large and growing, but no one was making an effort to convert users to washing powder. Nirma moved into this local vacuum.

Strategy #4: Recognize That Brands May Mean Something Completely Different

Global brands may lose something (or gain something) in translation. Brands that may stand for certain qualities in the developed world may have a completely different meaning in the developing world. Companies often expect their established brands to be greeted with open arms as a sign of development—and sometimes they are. But global brands may be virtually unknown in rural areas, conveying little advantage.

In many cases, the value added by a global brand is homogenized to one key value proposition—its foreignness. To the extent that this foreignness may add value, the brands may have value in developing markets, but for different reasons than in the developed market. For example, fast-food brands such as McDonald's, Pizza Hut, and KFC are considered upscale in developing markets. Their Western image raises the level of their brand among customers who want to be connected to the global village. This is contrary to their image and reputation in the developed world, where they are near the bottom of the food chain in luxury dining.

Because of these differences in how brands are interpreted, companies need to take care in rolling out brands in the developing world. Managers need to carefully assess what the brands mean in different regions.

Strategy #5: Address the Liabilities of Global Brands

While global brands appear to have many advantages—such as developed-world cachet and broad recognition—they also suffer from liabilities. Multinational companies need to address these liabilities, while local rivals may be able to benefit from them. For example, anti-American sentiments helped Mecca Cola challenge Coke and Pepsi among Muslim customers in Paris and other parts of the world, as well as aiding Quibla Cola in the UK and Zamzam Cola in Iran. These products are purchased by customers who like the appeal of cola but object to "Coca-Colonization."

The complexity of global and local branding can be seen in the success of Cola Turka in the Turkish soft drink market. This brand was launched in 2003 with advertising featuring U.S. actor Chevy Chase (popular in Turkey for his *National Lampoon* movies). It was a decidedly nationalistic brand promoted by an American celebrity who sang a traditional Turkish Boy Scout song and a Turkish-language version of "Take Me Out to the Ballgame" in advertising spots. This odd mix of local and global positioning led to a highly successful launch, provoking significant price cuts by Coca-Cola and Pepsi.

Global brands also have to be careful about attacks on local rivals and sensibilities. When a Toyota ad in a Chinese magazine showed a Toyota truck towing a Chinese rival up a muddy hill, Chinese customers were not amused by this direct attack on a local brand. Toyota apologized and pulled the ads. Similarly, a Nike television ad showing U.S. basketball player LeBron James defeating a cartoon kung fu master and a pair of dragons was banned by the government for offending the "national dignity."

Local brands sometimes are helped by local distribution networks and regulators, who favor local players. Government regulators often side with the local brands over large foreign rivals. For example, Chinese courts in Beijing ruled against Toyota when it charged that local competitor Geely had ripped off the Japanese car company's marquee. The court ruled that the logos were not that much alike and that consumers were not dumb enough to confuse Geely cars with pricier Japanese models.

Although it is important to recognize the impact of antiglobal and anti-American sentiments on the value of brands, this impact should not be overestimated. As protesters are throwing rocks at American fast-food restaurants, their compatriots are continuing to purchase dinner there. A 12-country study of 1,500 consumers by Douglas Holt, John Quelch, and Earl Taylor found that the "antiglobal" segment (not anti-American) constituted just 13 percent of the market. "Global citizens," who believe global brands signal high quality, made up 55 percent. "Global dreamers," who see global brands as a way to connect with the global village, accounted for 23 percent of the market.[5] This means that nearly 80 percent of the market continues to find value in global brands.

Strategy #6: Stretch Brands Without Breaking Them

Companies also need to be able to stretch their brands without breaking them. In 2004, Coke moved out of the major cities in China and India to push deeper into the smaller cities and towns, offering small bottles and low prices of about 12 U.S. cents per serving. The challenge was to address these markets without eroding its urban image. One Coca-Cola advertisement for rural Chinese markets shows a popular comic actor drinking Coca-Cola and closing the ad with a burp. The spot is in sharp contrast to its urban advertising, which positions Coke as a sophisticated drink for the rising middle class. While Pepsi has focused more on the cities, Coke holds a 55 percent share of Chinese sodas overall, compared to 27 percent for Pepsi. But will its more countrified image in rural areas erode the brand among urban customers?

Procter & Gamble was able to navigate this brand-stretching successfully in China. It moved its Crest toothpaste brand, which held more than half of the high-end segment by 2000, into the middle and low ends of the market. The company launched a cheaper, rural offering under the same brand, using cheaper ingredients, priced 30 percent below its premium brand. Its marketing emphasized cavity protection over the whiter teeth that were important in the premium segment. Crest's share of the middle market in China more than doubled from 5 percent to 12 percent from 2000 to 2002 while its premium products also increased market share from 5 to 8 percent.

Surrogate brands can also be used to stretch brands. Because of constraints on liquor and cigarette advertising in many parts of the world, companies have launched surrogate brands. The company can market soda or distilled water under the same brand as the alcohol. This builds awareness of the brand without violating rules against liquor advertising.

Religious restrictions often require creative solutions to branding. In Islamic countries, women's apparel, jewelry, and fashion accessories are advertised without using models because a woman's face cannot be shown. Advertisers work around this by showing silhouettes or women with their faces turned to the side, or they use Western models, because the restrictions don't apply to them. These ads can be creative and effective. While typical Western advertising focuses on diamonds and other jewelry as a sign of caring, such emotional appeals do not work in Islamic markets. Instead, jewelry is positioned as an expression of wealth, prosperity, and security. Dubai's Emirates Airline, using its central location to become one of the fastest-growing airlines in the world, has worked around concerns about hiring Muslim women as flight attendants by relying primarily on foreigners.

Strategy #7: Put the Brand on Wheels (or Legs)

To develop brands in rural villages, companies have used banner advertisements on elephants and video vans to build brand awareness. Colgate-Palmolive, for example, drives vans into rural villages to build brand and product category awareness. These vans, designed to introduce villagers in India to the concept of brushing teeth, show half-hour infomercials on the benefits of toothpaste and then distribute free samples.

Whereas the company might fight for a share of the supermarket shelves in cities or developed markets, in these rural villages, competition comes from local preparations made from charcoal powder and the neem tree. These local rivals have a significant advantage in distribution because their products can be found in the surrounding countryside. Companies also team up with nongovernmental organizations (NGOs) to promote toothbrushing or other aspects of personal hygiene by combining product promotion with social action. In media-deprived areas of the world, brands may rely much more on word of mouth and village leaders to develop the brand.

Brands on the Run

Branding in emerging markets defies simple formulas. These markets are neither entirely local nor entirely global, but a mix of global, national, and local brands. The success of small local brands can build new national and even global brands, such as Samsung, LG, and Haier. For certain segments and products, global brands are more appealing, but even these need to be positioned and tailored to local culture and tastes. The important thing is to recognize that markets tend to be more fragmented and branding and positioning more localized than in developed markets.

It may seem obvious that companies need to think about their branding strategy country by country and even local market by local market within countries. Companies need to develop a coherent portfolio of global and local brands. Such portfolios are apparent on the websites of companies with sophisticated global branding strategies, such as LG Electronics and Sony. They offer diverse home pages tailored to different countries showing different languages, customers, and products based on the country's specific needs. While LG Electronics' overall tagline "Life's good" is the same, what a "good life" means is interpreted market by market. In contrast to this extensive tailoring, some companies merely translate language or have only a local identity online.

The portfolio of global and local brands should be shaped by the company's brands and the demands and characteristics of specific markets within a given country. Companies need to become skilled at managing and balancing these complex portfolios based on insights from specific parts of the market. One key is to understand the roots of success for products and brands that are already successful in each market and to recognize that brands may have different meanings in these markets. What makes these brands attractive to this specific segment?

The 86 Percent Solution

- Examine how your brands, and those of competitors, are viewed in specific developing markets. What are their strong points, and what are their liabilities?

- Consider the distribution networks of developing markets and the advantages they may offer to local brands.

- Look for ways to transform or reinterpret your brands for local markets. What are the limits of stretching your brands? When can you reinvent them, and when do you need a new brand?

- If you need a new brand, examine whether you should acquire an existing brand or create a new one.

- Look for opportunities to build awareness of your brands in rural areas. Can you put your brands on wheels to penetrate media-deprived areas of the world?

Notes

1 Theodore Levitt. "The Globalization of Markets." *Harvard Business Review*, May–June 1983, pp. 2–11.

2 Rohit Saran with Malini Bhupta and Malini Goyal. "New Deals for Rural India." *India Today*, December 13, 2004.

3 Interview with the authors, 2004.

4 Speech by Sir John Bond, Goldman Sachs Conference, May 7, 2004, HSBC Holdings.

5 Douglas B. Holt, John A. Quelch, and Earl L. Taylor. "How Global Brands Compete." *Harvard Business Review*, September 2004.

5

THINK YOUNG

While the developed world is facing a crisis of aging, the 86 percent markets are a fountain of youth— although these youth may be different from their peers in developed countries. To understand this opportunity, companies have to think young.

Ramin looks across the table at his fiancée, Sogol, as they sip a morning cappuccino in a chic café in Tehran. She is careful not to get foam on the bandage on her nose, where she recently had plastic surgery. She adjusts her beautifully colored chador as she looks at Ramin. They are planning to go skiing next weekend at a resort in the Alborz Mountains in the north. He hopes she will be up to it. Ramin is just about to ask how she is recovering when his cellular phone vibrates. It is a text message from his boss, Kamel, at Pars-Online, one of the leading Internet service providers in Iran, calling him into the office to address a computer virus. His work with an online company puts him right at the intersection of cultural change, in the delicate crosshairs of the conflict between youthful revolution and tradition.

Although Ramin considers himself a devout Muslim, he holds some views that are quite different from those of his parents. Several of his colleagues have already left to take lucrative jobs in Europe, but he prefers to stay in Iran. One of his friends recently sent him an e-mail with a clip from the movie Marmoulak *(The Lizard). Although it won the best film award at Tehran's International Film Festival, the story of a thief disguised as a mullah was banned from Iranian theaters by religious leaders. Ramin wants to see the film, but he has a good job and likes being close to his family. And he expects things will continue to change.*

After work today, Ramin is planning to help his fiancée shop for a small dog before meeting some friends to go to a movie. Her parents don't understand keeping pets, which are considered unclean according to cultural and religious traditions, but she is infatuated with poodles. Ramin and Sogol are in their 20s. It will be another year before they are married, and it will be even longer before they have children, despite the pressure from their parents. He wants to move to a larger apartment and purchase a car. They have their eye on the new Logan from Romania but are also looking at the locally made Pecan. He looks with longing at a Mercedes going by on the street, but this is still out of their range. Someday, perhaps. They are in no hurry to grow up. They are enjoying being young.

Youth like Ramin and Sogol represent the future of developing markets. They are the majority of the population and are still growing. They are similar in some ways to youth in developed markets, but they are different in many ways. They are spending on fashion, education, technology, and even plastic surgery. How can you design products and services to meet this expanding young market? A huge opportunity exists for companies to think young.

MTV is one of the hallmarks of the youth culture. By recognizing both the differences and similarities of this youth culture in different parts of the world, MTV has become one of the most successful global entertainment companies. It's generated more than $1 billion in annual revenues outside the U.S. The entertainment giant initially tried to import its Western music and formats directly to India and other parts of the world. But MTV's programming didn't take off until it became a localized experience.

With rising local programming, nondomestic music now accounts for just 20 percent of MTV's music in India, down from 100 percent when the network was launched. Nonmusic programming is now entirely homegrown. MTV means something different in various parts of the world. In India, it broadcasts Bollywood music and humorous programming in Hindi, with hits such as a practical joke show called *MTV Bakra* (meaning "sacrificial lamb" or "goat"—in other words, the brunt of a joke). Chinese programs focus on family values and love songs. Indonesian MTV, catering to a large Islamic population, provides a call to prayer five times a day, and MTV Brazil has a salsa flavor. They all may "want their MTV," but it means something very different for each market.

MTV's common denominator is a focus on youth, but this means something different in the 140 countries it reaches through 31 localized television channels and 17 websites. "The cornerstone of success is relevance," said Alex Kuruvilla, managing director of MTV Networks India. "A lot of our research shows that you almost have to remind people that MTV is a global brand. Some of these markets have strong local cultures and sensitivities that you need to under-stand quite well."[1] Although *The Osbournes*, a reality television show focusing on an aging rock star and his family, didn't fly in India (view-ers couldn't relate), MTV did create a hit reality show called *Roadies* about a group of Indian youths who ride across India on motorbikes. They discover not just their country but each other.

Now products are flowing in both directions. Through its MTV World initiative, announced in December 2004, MTV is creating channels targeting Indian-American, Chinese-American, and Korean-American viewers in the U.S. MTV syndicates its Indian music segments in developed markets with large Indian populations.

Although culture is important in shaping MTV's image and pro-gramming in India, one of the biggest factors to consider is that most households with televisions (about 40 percent of the 200 million homes) have only a single set. This means that programming has to appeal to the target audience of 15 to 24 years old but not be offen-sive to parents, who control the remote. (It is a bit like programming a halftime show for the Super Bowl in U.S. football.) Fortunately, young Indians are less rebellious in their musical tastes than teens in the West, so the music is dominated by Bollywood hits that their par-ents can also appreciate. "The DNA of the brand is the 19-year-old, but it appeals to 'youthfulness' rather than 'youth,'" Kuruvilla said. "It is far more broad-based than in the U.S."

While the 86 percent markets may sometimes be culturally con-servative, they allow the company "to take risks and explore the unknown," he said. "Big surprises come in the form of successful ideas that have not been tried in other markets." For example, MTV created a credit card with Citibank, which became the fastest-growing cobranded card in India after its introduction four years ago.

Initially, the Indian market for MTV was considered a "niche business," Kuruvilla said. But youth markets in India and other emerging markets are far from niches. The youth *are* the market. Kuruvilla points out that, with more than half a billion Indians under the age of 25 and 700 million under 35, "That is a niche I'd like to have."

A Fountain of Youth

While the developed world is facing a crisis of aging, with pension and workforce challenges closing in on Japan and Europe in particular, the developing world is a fountain of youth. According to the United Nations, more than 100 countries had "youth bulges" in 2000, which means that young adults ages 15 to 29 make up more than 40 percent of adult populations, as shown in Figure 5-1. By 2015, India will have 550 million people under the age of 20—a population of youth and children that is twice the current size of the entire U.S. population.

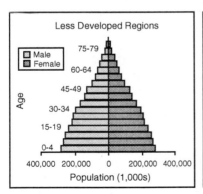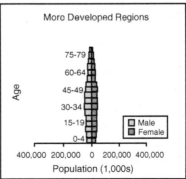

FIGURE 5-1   While many developed countries are dealing with declining workforces and increasing elderly populations, the developing world is facing a youth bulge that will add nearly one billion people to the global labor force over the next decade. (Source: Population Resource Center, 2004)

Developing countries will account for about 90 percent of the increases in world population through 2050, growing 14 times faster than developed countries, according to the Population Reference Bureau. Although Europe's population is expected to drop by about 60 million people by mid-century, China will increase by about 100 million, India by about 500 million, and Africa by 900 million. In this period, Ethiopia and The Democratic Republic of Congo will join the list of the top 10 most populous countries, and Russia and Japan will drop off.

These populations are already young, as shown in Figure 5-2. In 2004, more than 40 percent of Iraq's population was under 15, with a median age across the country of about 19. Half the Nigerian population is under 15, compared to just 14 percent in Japan.

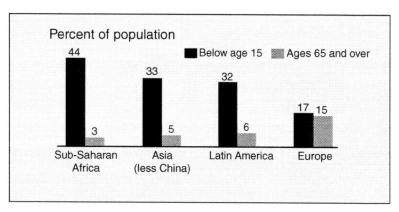

FIGURE 5-2 While children and youth under 15 greatly outnumber the elderly (over 65) in Sub-Saharan Africa and Asia (without China), these populations are nearly equal in Europe. (Source: Population Reference Bureau, 2004 World Population Data Sheet)

The one exception to the youth trend among developing countries is China. Its one-child-per-couple policy has put the brakes on its population growth, reducing average fertility rates from 5.8 children in 1970 to 1.8 children in 2004. The Chinese population is expected to age in one generation as much as Europe's did in a century. By 2015, China's median age of 44 will be higher than in the U.S., and by mid-century, the Asian giant will be shedding 20 to 30 percent of its population per year. (China has recently relaxed this policy, allowing some couples to have two children.) But, in the meantime, what will be the impact of all these doting grandparents on their only grand-children? These *xiao huangdi*, or "little emperors," are bemoaned as self-centered and spoiled by doting parents and grandparents, but this creates significant markets for products tailored to these young emperors. As they grow up, how will each of these children be able to support two aging parents and four aging grandparents?

Growth of the Core Consuming Class

These demographic shifts have significant implications for the growth of the population in the core consuming class of 25 to 44 in the years ahead. A study by Christopher Woods of Credit Lyonnaise Securities Asia (CLSA) examined the implications of the 1 billion baby boomers in Asia, including China and India. As with the baby boom in the U.S., these increasingly affluent Asian boomers will be the driving force behind spending and market growth in ways that will "drive world economic growth for the next decade or two." Woods also points out that the baby boom in the U.S. led to other changes that might also be seen in Asia. As baby boomers came of age, they moved out of their parents' homes, creating a huge demand for housing, appliances, and other products. Household formation began to increase faster than the growth of the population. Just as the U.S. baby boomers drove the growth of the U.S. economy after World War II, these Asian boomers will drive economic growth across Asia. For governments, these exploding populations present tremendous chal-lenges, but for businesses, they create opportunities.

Among developed countries, only the U.S. will post significant overall population growth in the first 50 years of the millennium, rising by 43 percent, driven in large part by high rates of immigration (as dis-cussed in Chapter 3, "Aim for the Ricochet Economy"). Even so, the

U.S. youth population (under 18) is expected to drop from 26 percent in 2000 to 24 percent in 2020. With rising elderly populations and fewer workers to support them, other developed countries are considering opening the floodgates to immigration, which will pose serious cultural challenges in Europe and particularly in Japan. In the developed world, Japanese automakers such as Nissan and Toyota have been designing new models for an expanding population of elderly drivers. They feature amenities such as swivel seats and a motorized crane to lift a wheelchair into the trunk. Senior citizens are showing up on U.S. college campuses in increasing numbers, and maternity wards in Germany are feeling the pinch from the country's declining birthrate. But in developing markets, the opportunities are in the opposite direction. How can companies take advantage of this youth bulge to build their businesses?

Strategies for the Youth Market

What opportunities does the youthfulness of emerging markets create? How can companies capitalize on these opportunities? The following sections discuss several strategies for tapping into the youthfulness of the 86 percent markets.

Strategy #1: Focus on Youthful Products and Services

The rising young population of the developing world is creating a market for mobile phones, education, games, computers, entertainment, apparel, fast food, cafés, fashion, colored contact lenses, magazines, and music. An MTV survey of more than 2,000 Indian youth in 2004 found that the "coolest things to have" were small and latest-model cell phones, perfume and deodorants, cash, car and bike keys, jewelry, a credit card, a Walkman or Discman, and a laptop computer. Appearance was also quite important, with neatly combed hair considered cool by 38 percent of respondents and sleek gelled hair considered cool by 33 percent.[2]

The Chinese spend $2.4 billion every year on plastic surgery and other beauty treatments, coming in third after real estate and vacations. This trend would have been unthinkable a generation ago. It represents the value that young people in China are placing on individualism and youth. It is also seen as a way to enhance occupational and social success. Taiwanese salon chain Natural Beauty operates 1,522 franchised stores in China, focusing on customers aged 25 to 39. China has even held its first beauty contest among women who have undergone the surgery. Can a Chinese version of the popular makeover show *The Swan* be far behind?

Cell phones, the hallmark of youth culture around the globe, have grown rapidly, becoming the biggest-selling product in the world. Nokia, which is setting up a new plant in India, expects that 80 percent of its new mobile customers between now and 2007 will come from the developing world. Young customers help drive applications such as polyphonic ring tones, digital cameras, gaming, and text messaging, which keep customers purchasing new equipment.

Chinese beverage maker Wahaha, which built a billion-dollar business under the noses of Coca-Cola and PepsiCo by penetrating rural markets, uses the slogan "Youth knows no failure." It announced plans in 2004 to expand its brand beyond beverages to the fast-growing market for children's clothing.

Music and entertainment appeal to youth around the globe. When Viacom continued to expand its distribution in China through a partnership with Beijing Television to broadcast music and entertainment, Chairman and CEO Sumner Redstone remarked that "There is no limit to our appetite here." The company will continue to grow where the youth culture is growing the fastest. News Corporation's StarTV launched a youth-focused Chinese game show called *Women in Control*, with men on the stage and women as judges, a sign that media is beginning to relax. The expanding role of media has led to rising advertising revenues in China, which reached $7 billion in 2003 (still small compared to the more than $100 billion spent in the U.S.).

Entertainment is increasingly focused on youth from developing countries. Interest is increasing in the Miss World competition, which was held in Beijing and was won by Miss Peru in 2004, with runners-up including women from China, India, and the Philippines. Korean soap operas are a big hit across Asia. Stars such as Bae Yong-joon and Choi Ji-woo, on the popular show *Winter Sonata*, have developed a cult following even in Japan, which typically has not looked to Korea for romance and fashion. The shows have also sparked an upsurge in Korean tourism as fans seek out the locations shown in the episodes.

Romance is a popular subject of Bollywood films. An example is the 2004 movie *Veer-Zaara*, a love story between an Indian man and a Pakistani woman. Although the taboos they challenge may be different, the youth of the developing world, like all youth, are pushing the limits of tradition and culture. In 2004, Disney and TimeWarner launched five new children's cable channels in Asia. They joined the four already broadcasting in more than half a dozen languages—an indication of expanding cable penetration and an interest in reaching Asian youth.

Strategy #2: Understand Who Controls the Remote

Even though young people may dominate the populations of developing markets, they may not have the most political and economic power. As mentioned earlier, while MTV may appeal to youth, Indian parents in one-television households still control the remote. As companies push the limits to appeal to young markets, they need to be aware of the strong countervailing forces of culture and tradition from the older generation. In the developing world, the tolerance for those who challenge social norms is typically a bit lower than in the developed world.

For example, in 2004, after a kiss was shown on a Middle Eastern version of the British hit program *Big Brother*, the show was pulled after only two episodes. The show was a sanitized version of the bawdy British broadcast, in which six men and six women vied for a $100,000 prize while living together in a house over three months. In the version filmed in Bahrain, the men and women were housed in separate quarters, with their own prayer rooms. No filming occurred in the women's bedrooms, and no physical contact was allowed, as in the UK version. Yet even this watered-down version brought 1,000 protesters into the streets after a woman and man exchanged a social kiss on the cheek in the first episode. After the protests, which reflected growing resentment over the lax morals of television programming, the local broadcaster quickly pulled the show from the air. Young people can challenge their traditions, but the older generation might strike back. Those who market to youth in the developing world need to pay close attention to these dynamics.

It is important to recognize that some of the greatest increases in populations in the developing world are among more stringent religious groups. For example, the Indian census in 2000 showed that over the prior decade, India added 180 million Hindus and 50 million Muslims to the population. Muslims have the highest fertility rates of any group in India. This means that many of the new global youth in developing countries may be very far removed from the youth culture of the developed world.

Strategy #3: Appeal to Youth with "Dual Passports"

Saudi Arabian entertainment company Rotana, the largest distributor of Arab songs, has struck a delicate balance between the demands of local culture and the desires of a growing youth market. Its 24-hour cable music channel pauses the undulating dancers at prayer times to show a still image and a serious religious message. And then the music starts again. Although the program is free for viewers, in contrast to cable offerings, the company makes money on advertising and the 20,000 text messages exchanged by viewers every day. Founder Al-Waleed bin Talal, a member of the Saudi royal family, is aiming to build a Middle Eastern entertainment giant by serving what he jokingly calls a "niche" youth market—60 percent of the population.

The youth in these markets hold what Elissa Moses has called "dual passports." Moses, in a 1997 study of 27,000 teens in 44 countries, found that although young people are plugged into their local culture and religion, they also share common tastes for global culture such as music, fashion, film, video games, and technology. Among global characteristics are a strong sense of individualism leading to a focus more on themselves than their communities. A study by Roper ASW of Asian teens ages 13 to 19 found that they ranked individualism, ambition, freedom, and other values significantly higher than adults between 40 and 65.

Video games such as Nintendo's "Pokemon" and Take-Two Interactive's "Grand Theft Auto" have attracted a global following among young players. Cartoon characters such as SpongeBob SquarePants and the Powerpuff Girls are playing across Asia, where only about 20 percent of children's programming is locally developed. To understand some of the products these global youth may be interested in, consider the young Echo Boomers or Generation Y, who accounted for nearly a third of the U.S. population in 2004. They spend their own and their parents' money on brands such as Sony, Patagonia, Gap, and Aveda.

On the other hand, global culture can succeed with a surprisingly local aspect. While these youth may watch movies, listen to MTV, drink Coke, and eat fast food at McDonald's, it is important to recognize that these activities, although they appear similar, may mean different things in different parts of the world. Self-help guru Deepak Chopra and director Shekhar Kapur have joined forces to create Gotham Studios Asia, which is developing comic books for Indian audiences. For example, a version of *Spider-Man* is set in Mumbai, with Pavitr Pabhakar replacing Peter Parker. A mysterious yogi is substituted for the radioactive spider that gives Pavitr his powers, and a demon from Indian mythology replaces the villainous Green Goblin. *Sesame Street* has developed locally tailored shows in more than 20 countries, using local stories, settings, and songs to create Takalani Sesame in South Africa, Alam Simsim in Egypt, Ulitsa Sezam in Russia, and Zhima Jie in China. Youth want to connect with global themes and brands, but they still want them to feel local.

Strategy #4: Understand the Influencers

Youth markets may be driven by different influencers than more mature segments. The top influencers for new trends among Indian youth were friends, ahead of television, music channels, retail stores, and film stars. MTV's study of Indian youth found that while Bollywood films were the top source of new fashion trends, there were many other sources around the world. Some 67 percent looked to Hollywood films, 59 percent turned to Paris, 42 percent looked to the U.S., and 55 percent looked to foreign shows such as *Friends*. Others look to Indian designers, VJs from music channels, and local designers.

Young buyers worldwide have a skeptical view of packaged messages. They are less easily reached through mass media. But they are heavily influenced by word of mouth, movie stars, cricket players, musicians, and the Internet. They also tend to get out and shop more, particularly with smaller homes. Campaigns targeting youth in developed markets offer insights into the different approaches to youth segments. In 2004, Toyota launched a new car division, Scion, to target young U.S. consumers, spending 70 percent of its promotion on street events rather than television and Internet ads to build the brand. Even advertising for these audiences tends to be more straightforward, unflinching, and edgy. While advertising for feminine products has traditionally been discreet, new U.S. ads targeting younger women are much more bold. A Tampax commercial shows a girl plugging a hole in her canoe with a tampon, and Kotex uses a red dot with the slogan "Kotex fits. Period." Approaches that might have been considered shocking a generation ago are now considered vital to breaking through to young customers. Youth in developing markets may require similar innovations.

Strategy #5: Appeal to Parents

High birthrates and growing incomes naturally lead to a booming market for products for babies, children, and their parents. There will be opportunities to sell products such as disposable diapers, toys, video games, and entertainment directed at young children. Disney will open a new Disneyland theme park in Hong Kong in 2005, and Universal Studios announced plans for a theme park in Shanghai in 2006, at the center of rapidly growing Asian economies. Isn't there an opportunity to create a global chain of childcare facilities for developing countries?

The most successful offerings are those that can involve the whole family. For example, moviegoers are not used to taking children to children's movies. The movie *Spider-Man* was a big hit in India because both parents and children wanted to see it. Many other opportunities exist to expand or create businesses targeted to parents and their young children.

Strategy #6: Recognize Opportunities for Education

A growing and upwardly mobile youth market in developing countries is creating an expanding market for education. Elementary and secondary education have grown rapidly, as have tutoring programs, because parents want to ensure that their children have the education to participate in the benefits of economic development. Private educational services have filled the growing need for education from preschool through college by filling in the gaps left by underfunded government-run schools. In India, parents pay up to 30,000 rupees (US$670) to prepare their children for the crucial tenth standard exams. Mumbai alone has an estimated 1,000 such coaching classes.

The demand for a college education also has been growing. For example, 17 percent of all students in Swiss and Australian universities are foreign. However, international enrollments in U.S. graduate programs are declining due to visa restrictions and growing foreign competition. This has raised concerns in the U.S. Microsoft founder Bill Gates, for example, has said that the 35 percent drop in Asian students in U.S. computer science programs due to tougher visa rules is threatening U.S. competitiveness in computer software. Many new business schools and other professional schools have been established in China, India, and other developing nations to meet the need for high-level knowledge. Kellogg and Wharton helped launch the Indian School of Business in Hyderabad, India, and they also collaborated in establishing the Sasin business school in Thailand. Even so, of the top 100 full-time global MBA programs identified by the *Financial Times* in 2005, only about half a dozen were from developing countries. INSEAD created a new campus in Singapore, and the European Union has joined with the Chinese government to establish the China Europe International Business School in Shanghai. In 2004, Harvard University set up a medical school in Dubai. Cornell University's Weill Medical College created a school in Qatar, in the midst of the developing countries of the Middle East and South Asia.

Technology can help increase the reach of such programs. For example, schools are offering e-learning programs at university campuses across China. The World Bank's World Links program has offered technology to underprivileged schools in more than 20 nations that have connected thousands of students and teachers with online educational resources. The United Nations Development Programme (UNDP), operating in 167 countries, has created a Virtual Development Academy to offer training to personnel from developing agencies, donors, government counterparts, and civil society in developing countries.

Other technologies can also facilitate education. LeapFrog Enterprises built a $680 million business with electronic learning toys such as the LeapPad. Children can touch a pen to words in a book and hear the words spoken, helping them develop reading skills. In August 2004, the U.S. Department of Health and Human Services announced plans to purchase 20,000 LeapPads to be used in Afghanistan to improve health-care knowledge in a country in which 80 percent of the women are illiterate. The LeapPads, programmed to speak in the two most common languages, will educate rural women about the benefits of immunization and the dangers of sexually transmitted diseases. If the pilot in Afghanistan is successful, it could be applied to AIDS education and other health-care initiatives in other parts of the world.

Strategy #7: Follow the Migration into the Cities

With increasing urbanization, most of the young people in developing countries will be living in cities. By 2007, for the first time in human history, more of the world's population will be living in cities than in rural areas. By 2030, some 60 percent of the planet could reside in urban areas.[2] The urban population in Nigeria, for example, increased from 14 percent to 44 percent between 1970 and 2000. In the same period, South Korea's cities swelled from 28 percent to 88 percent of the population.

By 2004, China had more than 100 million migrant workers, many of whom came from rural areas seeking work opportunities. Most of this "floating population" was drawn from the rural elite, younger and better educated than those who remained behind. Their remittances sent home are among the biggest source of wealth for rural villages. This upwardly mobile population in China and other developing markets, while different from their wealthier peers who were born in the cities, can represent a significant market if they are successful in moving up from entry-level factory jobs to better-paying opportunities. These new urban immigrants, many of them young women between 18 and 25, get cut off from their roots. This has led to some reverse migration back to the rural villages.

Strategy #8: Understand the Changing Roles of Women

The changes brought about by youth culture are felt perhaps most intensely by young women. In the early development of markets, companies often do not pay much attention to women, but this changes over time as companies create products and marketing campaigns for women. This has become a huge market in the developed world, with companies such as Volvo creating cars specially designed for women and other firms developing innovations in products from feminine hygiene to razors. Similar changes are happening in developing markets, and youth are helping drive these changes.

With access to global values, these women may want to leave behind the restrictions on their education and careers in cultures that offer women few opportunities. At the same time, they will face opposition from the older generation, and they have few role models. When *Fortune* magazine in 2004 listed the 50 most influential women outside the U.S., only about a quarter were from developing countries, and many had assumed control of family businesses from their parents or husbands. A 2004 *Wall Street Journal* list of top women executives included only about half a dozen working for companies based in developing countries. The developed world has a limited number of role models for women in business, and most parts of the developing world have even fewer such role models.

Shifts in the role of young women create opportunities for companies that can follow these shifts. Hindustan Lever's Fair & Lovely became the top-selling skin cream in India after its launch in 1975 by meeting a growing demand for "fairness products" in Asia (products that lighten skin tone—not to white, but to a lighter shade). Millions of women in India used the product as an all-purpose beauty cream with a promise of fairness, viewed as a way to be more attractive and marriageable, since marriage was seen as the ultimate goal for a young woman. As opportunities for women increased, however, this positioning began losing power by the late 1990s, as competitors such as Fairever began taking market share.

Therefore, in 2001 Fair & Lovely made a dramatic change in its positioning and emotional payoff, moving away from offering romance and marriage focus instead on women's economic empowerment. In 2003, Fair & Lovely also initiated a series of activities to promote women's economic empowerment through its Fair & Lovely Foundation, which provides scholarships, career fairs, and skill development for women.

By recognizing the shift in the views of Indian women, from a primary focus on marriage to a concern for economic empowerment, Fair & Lovely was able to reposition and re-energize its product across Asia. This shift, along with new ayurvedic "anti-marks" and "deep skin" formulations launched between 2002 and 2004, helped give the brand 42 percent share of the total skin care market in India. Taking note of women's rising incomes, Fair & Lovely also launched a premium brand, Perfect Radiance from Fair & Lovely, which moved it into competition with top brands such as Garnier and Revlon.

Youth Leads to Growth

The youthfulness of developing markets creates opportunities. The hundreds of millions of people who will be born in developing markets in the coming decades will define the markets of tomorrow. Companies that recognize and tailor products to these youthful segments, while appreciating how they differ from youth in developed markets, will create significant businesses today and will lay the foundation for future growth as these customers mature. (At the same time, we cannot overlook that these 86 percent markets still have populations of older citizens that are larger than those of developed countries.)

In the next half century, the empowerment of women and increasing urbanization are expected to end the youth bulge and therefore the development of these markets. By 2050, experts predict a "birth dearth," with the global population aged 60 and older exceeding the population of youth under 15 worldwide for the first time. But before this birth dearth begins (if it happens at all), a generation or more of young people will dominate developing markets. These youth will define the products and brands that will be successful in global markets. The companies that appeal to them today will create the brands these consumers recognize as they grow up. To grow with these markets, companies need to think young.

The 86 Percent Solution

- Consider the products, services, and strategies that will appeal most to the youthful markets of the developing world.

- Explore the specific ways in which the youth in emerging markets differ from their counterparts in the developed world. What do these differences mean for your products and services in different developing markets?

- Examine the attitudes, traditions, and religious influences on youth in the markets you are in or entering. How will these factors limit the typical rebellion of youth?

- Identify who controls the youth market's remote control and purse strings. What impact will parents and others have on opportunities?

- Look for possibilities to market products to young parents and small children, particularly educational products.

- Find the influencers such as entertainers or fashion leaders in your markets. How can you use these influencers to expand your markets for your products and services?

- Look for opportunities in the changing roles of women in developing markets. Can you expand your markets while empowering young women?

Notes

1 Interview, August 31, 2004.

2 UNFPA. "State of the World Population 2004," p. 23. http://www.unfpa.org/swp/2004/pdf/en_swp04.pdf.

6

GROW BIG BY THINKING SMALL

While the developed world may want to be super-sized, big successes in developing markets often come in small packages. Small payments, sachets, and products tailored to small spaces can create big opportunities.

In a small shop in Karachi, Pakistan, Fatima makes her way through the shops near the Bohri Bazaar. The middle-aged housewife purchases her daily vegetables and other groceries from the same stores that her mother frequented and prepares her meals according to the same recipes. But she also stops at a small health and beauty aids store to pick up a 5 ml sachet of Procter & Gamble's Herbal Essences shampoo for 3 rupees (about 5 U.S. cents). She had been using Kala Kola's Bioamla ever since she started buying shampoo. She is now interested in trying this new Western brand, which offers what its marketing calls "a uniquely satisfying experience."

Although the 200 ml bottle of Herbal Essences is designed to evoke the jars of ancient drugstores, and its oval shape shows its harmony with nature, Fatima is unimpressed. She has no room for this huge bottle in their small apartment. She also is in the habit of purchasing her food and other essentials every day, so it makes sense to buy her sachets of shampoo when she needs them.

Fatima and her husband, Shafiq, after paying off an LG television, recently bought a small refrigerator from RMPLC by signing up for a series of small payments. Now, she doesn't absolutely have to shop every day, but she wouldn't feel like she was taking care of her family if she let her duties slip. Still, she is thankful for the small comforts and pleasures of life, such as trying this new shampoo.

Customers such as Fatima have made single-use packages, or sachets, one of the hottest innovations in developing markets. Hindustan Lever's sachets account for about half of its more than $2 billion sales in the Indian subcontinent— roughly equal to the revenues of IT services giant Infosys. And these revenues are all the more remarkable because they were achieved a few pennies at a time. With tight incomes and small living quarters, developing-market customers are buying sachets and other small purchases to fill their "just-in-time" pantries. Small apartments and incomes also create opportunities for other innovations. How can you rethink your payments, products, and packaging to grow big by thinking small?

CavinKare's Chik shampoo became a rural powerhouse in southern India thanks to the innovation of low-priced sachets of shampoo. While shampoo brands such as Clinic Plus and Sunsilk fought for urban mindspace in India, CavinKare turned its attention to the needs of rural markets, designing products to reach them. CavinKare's research in the early 1980s showed that the idea of using shampoo was becoming more accepted in rural and small-town markets. The studies showed that, on average, about five adults in each household washed their hair once a week. This was a market waiting to happen.

Pricing was a problem, however. A typical sachet priced at 2 rupees (4 U.S. cents) would lead to a total cost of 8 rupees (16 cents) per person for four washes a month, which was more than these rural consumers were willing to pay. The company's surveys found that if the *monthly* cost could be cut to 2 rupees (4 cents), consumers would be willing to try shampoo instead of bath soap to wash their hair. CavinKare worked backward from these numbers to launch its Chik shampoo in 50-paise (1-cent) sachets in 1983. In one year, the brand sold about 1 million sachets in the Indian state of Tamil Nadul. The next year, Chik was launched in the neighboring southern states of Andhra Pradesh and Karnataka.

Sachets and small packets of products such as shampoos, detergents, tea, coffee, and chocolates have been a huge success in emerging markets. Unilever sells Rexona deodorant sticks for 16 cents and up, helping it grab 60 percent of the market in India, the Philippines, Bolivia, and Peru. In Nigeria, a tube with enough Close Up toothpaste for 20 brushings sells for about 8 cents. Unilever offers 3-inch-square packets of margarine that don't require refrigeration, addressing both the desire for small packages and the weaknesses in infrastructure (as discussed in Chapter 7, "Bring Your Own Infrastructure"). Across all companies in the Philippines, sachets of personal care and cleaning products accounted for as much as 95 percent of total sales.

In the U.S., a bigger-is-better mind-set led Wal-Mart to offer a gallon of Vlasic pickles (12 pounds) for less than $3, and fast-food restaurants routinely offer to "super size" for a small charge. But the developing world is selling cigarettes one at a time in hole-in-the-wall shops.

Inverted Pricing

The logic of pricing these sachets is turned on its head in developing markets because consumers actually pay less per volume for small packages. In India, Hindustan Lever charges 87 percent more per unit for its 5,000-gram Surf Excel family pack compared to the per-unit price of sachets. Similarly, Procter & Gamble charges an 80 percent premium for its family-size package of Tide compared to the same amount of detergents in sachets.

In contrast, consumers in developed markets pay more at a convenience store to purchase a single serving of soda versus a 2-liter bottle because they want a quick drink. They purchase a small bag of chips rather than family size because they want something that is convenient to eat at lunch without repackaging. Generally these consumers in the developed world pay a premium for the convenience of a readily available small package and are given discounts for buying in volume through family size-packages or 2-liter bottles. The idea is to encourage customers to purchase higher volumes, which are less expensive to produce.

The pricing in developing markets at first appears to be counterintuitive. But there is a different motivation for small packages in developed and developing markets. In developed markets, consumers buy small packages for *convenience* and are willing to pay a premium for this. In the developing world, consumers buy smaller packages for *price* because of limited resources or a desire to conserve money and independence. These consumers are not choosing between a large and a small package but whether to buy the product at all. A consumer who may not be able to afford a family-size package can afford a sachet.

How can companies afford to offer smaller packages for a lower price? It obviously costs more to make and sell many small packages than one large one. The answer is that companies focus on economies of volume rather than economies of scale, growing the market for their products. The sachet sales do not cannibalize sales of larger packages. Instead, they attract new customers who might not otherwise buy the product. Therefore, low-priced sachets are not cutting into the business of their larger packages, as they might in a developed country. Developing countries also have cost advantages in manufacturing and sales that can translate to lower prices. For example, the average hourly cost of Chinese factory labor is just 64 cents, compared to about $21.11 in the U.S.

Small Homes

The population density (population per square kilometer) of Karachi, Pakistan, is about 10 times as high as New York City. Mumbai is more than 7 times, Manila is almost 6 times, Shanghai is nearly 3 times, and Mexico City is about 2.5 times as densely populated as New York. According to avid Indian art collector and industrialist Harsh Goenka, one of the reasons people don't buy sculptures in Mumbai is because homes are so small that they have no room for art. In fact, one sculptor who produced 11 works for a Mumbai show destroyed the eight unsold sculptures at the end of the show because there was no place to store them.[1] Homes are smaller in urban areas because of crowded conditions and are smaller in rural areas because of low incomes.

The average size of a house in the U.S., which grew by 38 percent between 1975 and 2000, is about 2,200 square feet. This is about twice the size of houses in Japan and Europe and 26 times the living space of the average person in Africa. In Nairobi, Kenya, where slum dwellers constitute 60 percent of the population but occupy only 5 percent of the land, a typical home might be 150 square feet. (Some 924 million people worldwide lived in slums in 2001, with overcrowded housing and unhealthy living conditions.)

In Peter Menzel's 1995 book *Material World*, based on data from the United Nations and World Bank, he offers portraits of average families around the developing world. These include a family of 13 (plus livestock) in Bhutan living in a 726-square-foot dwelling, a family of 9 in Cuba living in 1,400 square feet, a family of 11 in Mali living in 990 square feet, a family of 9 in China living in 600 square feet, a family of 6 in India living in 344 square feet, and a family of 5 in Guatemala living in 216 square feet. This is compared to a U.S. family of four living in a 1,600-square-foot home.[2] To make matters worse, housing regulations that make it difficult for landlords to evict tenants have left apartments vacant despite housing shortages. Owners are reluctant to take on the burden of tenants for life.

Strategies for Thinking Small

How can companies grow big by thinking small? A number of "small" strategies can lead to big success.

Strategy #1: Fill the Just-in-Time Pantry

Even when consumers can afford a larger package, an environment of scarcity means that most want to hold on to their wallets. Some consumers in developing countries, for example, do not fill their gas tanks even when they can afford to do so. The cash in their pockets is much more flexible than the fuel in their tanks. The same holds true for a bottle of shampoo or box of soap. Why tie up precious resources in inventory?

Developing-world residents prefer a "just-in-time" approach to stocking their smaller pantries and the many small neighborhood stores. Small packages allow them to buy only what they need, making frequent small purchases rather than infrequent large ones. Who wants to tie up the precious shelf space in a small house with an oversized box of detergent? In this environment, the "buy one, get one free" strategy is ineffective. Where would the customer put the second box? (Actually, customers could sell it to their neighbors through ad hoc demand pooling, as discussed in the section "Strategy #5: Join Many Small Drops to Make an Ocean.") Instead, the pantry is filled as needed, so smaller packages are an advantage, even if cost is not an issue (as it often is). There is no space in the refrigerator, or no refrigerator at all. In general, consumers do not buy ahead except in cases where they want to stay ahead of rapid inflation or anticipated shortages in the market. In addition, in societies in which wastage is considered taboo, it is better to buy too little than too much.

Not just household products benefit from small packages. Cemex has become one of the leading producers and marketers of cement and ready-mix products in the world, in large part by selling small bags of cement to individual homeowners. Small bags allow for modular homebuilding on limited budgets. The average low-income homeowner in Mexico typically takes four years to complete one room, at a total cost of US$1,500, usually one 110-pound bag of cement at a time. It takes about 13 years to complete a four-room home. Cemex created a program called Patrimonio Hoy in 1999 to reach these low-income customers, helping them save (often through community-based savings groups, called *tandas*) and offering advice that reduced the time and cost of building. Within three years, the program had tripled the amount of cement consumed by low-income home builders, and more than 13,000 Mexican families had participated.

Programs such as this are helping Cemex grow its business in developing countries such as Bangladesh, Egypt, Indonesia, Thailand, the Philippines, and other parts of the world. Cemex projections show that while cement sales in developed countries will grow by 1 percent annually through 2010, developing countries will post 4 percent growth. Do-it-yourself cement sales account for 40 percent of all sales in Mexico, with a potential market that Cemex estimates at $500 to $600 million in that country alone. Cemex's home market in Mexico contributed 70 percent of the company's profits in 2003, even though it accounted for only 37 percent of sales.

Strategy #2: Use Small Payments

Magazine Luiza's has become the third-largest Brazilian retailer by assiduously courting the poor. These stores make 80 percent of their sales on credit, offering small installment payments to low-income customers. Products are priced based on the size of payments, not the total cost. While this might seem like a very risky strategy, the default rate of Magazine Luiza's customers is very low, about 50 percent below the average across all Brazilian retailers. Every time customers come into the store to make their small installment payments, they see discount appliances, furniture, or other goods.

To penetrate more rural areas, Magazine Luiza set up virtual stores, showrooms with banks of computers offering online access to the company's inventory with home delivery guaranteed in 48 hours. The cost of setting up these stores was 15 percent of the investment in a conventional store. These stores also offered online education and banking services. Through small payments, Magazine Luiza has risen from a small department store chain to a retail powerhouse. Even during the down cycles of Brazil's notoriously volatile economy, the company has posted strong growth, reaching sales of more than $400 million in 2004.

Similarly, Indonesian retailer Ramayana Lestari Sentosa has built a vibrant business by focusing on low-income and rural customers. Brazilian retailer Casas Bahia became Brazil's biggest nonfood retailer, selling about $8 billion reais (US$2.9 billion) in furniture, household goods, and appliances through about 400 stores in 2004, based on small payments by low-income customers.

Banks are also recognizing that low-income borrowers can be the basis of profitable businesses. Through its Banamex division, Citigroup has pushed banking deeper into the villages and lower-income segments of Mexico, where only one in five citizens has a bank account. Citigroup found in 2001 that only 12 percent of Mexican purchases were made using credit and debit cards, compared to more than half of all purchases in the U.S. To change this pattern, the company is working with employers to arrange to pay employees through payroll cards, prepaid cards that can be used like debit cards in ATMs or for purchases. Citigroup's expansion is made one small payroll card and one small village banking window at a time. But these small initiatives add up. Credit card profit margins are healthy—Citigroup's international margins are about double what it earns in the U.S.—and the company's Mexican operations earn more than $1 billion per year. (Whether encouraging credit and higher-interest installments in the developing world is a good development in the long run is still an open question. Proponents argue that it gives people access to a higher standard of living, and opponents argue that some businesses take advantage of the poor.)

Getting in on the ground floor of these low-income markets also offers companies a relationship with middle-class consumers as they emerge. Of course, developing markets are heterogeneous, with diverse income levels and segments, but the high concentration of low-income customers drives smaller thinking. While the developed world may be used to buying cars or homes on installment payments, the developing world applies this same model to much smaller products, such as bicycles and small appliances.

Microlending (discussed in Chapter 1, "The Lands of Opportunity") has also demonstrated the power of small payments. Although many microlending initiatives started out as charitable organizations, most are now self-sufficient and have spawned a number of for-profit lenders around the world. For example, Accion is a private nonprofit organization that provides microloans to the self-employed poor in Latin American, Africa, and other parts of the world. It has helped create a number of fully commercial microfinance institutions, including BancoSol in Bolivia, Mibanco in Peru, SogeSol in Haiti, Banco Solidario in Ecuador, and Financiera Compartamos in Mexico. In 1996, BancoSol alone crossed the $1 million mark in earnings. A year later, it became the first microfinance institution to issue dividends to shareholders. In 2004, Accion distributed a total of $1.76 billion to nearly 1.5 million entrepreneurs around the world.

Strategy #3: Combine Products to Conserve Space

Smaller homes create a demand for creative housing designs that make spaces look bigger and convey a sense of privacy in crowded apartments. Cramped quarters also create markets for space-saving appliances and furniture. This is why many middle-class Indians have refrigerators made by South Korea's Samsung. Designing for the tight apartments of Seoul, where the population density is more than 4,000 people per square kilometer, the company has learned to tailor its products to narrow dwellings. Smaller homes also mean that residents spend more of their time in shops or public spaces.

Because of space constraints, companies often succeed by combining several products in a single package. Microsoft has developed an entertainment system that combines a television, computer, DVD player, and stereo. While it is designed for the convenience of consumers in the developed world who are juggling too many remote controls, such products could also be very attractive in the small homes of developing markets as a way to save space. Professor Raj Reddy at Carnegie Mellon University is working on a $250 combination wireless networked PC-TV-DVD-phone, which should be available by 2006. It is targeted at the 4 billion people living on less than $2,000 per year.

Many other combinations might not be as obvious as Microsoft's entertainment system. For example, LG is putting flat-panel televisions and Internet connections into its high-end refrigerators in the

U.S. Wouldn't a cheaper version of this combination (a television in a low-end refrigerator) also be of interest to the developing world, as their primary television or computer? In the Preface, we mentioned the idea of combining a toilet and a computer. This might be an unsettling image from a developed-market perspective, but for a consumer in a small shanty just moving into the era of indoor plumbing, this is not such a far-fetched idea. If washers and dryers can be combined, what other product combinations could be used to meet multiple needs while conserving space?

In addition to taking up less space in a crowded apartment, such combination products would typically cost less than buying the individual components. While consumers in developed markets might already own some of these products, leading to replacement costs, many consumers in the developing world are buying all three products for the first time. This makes such combinations particularly attractive.

These bundled products not only save space and cost but also can facilitate market adoption. For example, in many parts of the developing world, washing machines are catching on, but dryers have been slow to be adopted. People still dry their clothes in the sun, because clothes from the dryer don't smell as fresh. One way to overcome this is to combine washers and dryers into a single appliance.

Alternatively, companies can design larger products that are modular, which makes them easy to move in and out of small apartments or houses. One of Chinese appliance maker Haier's early successes was a refrigerator-freezer that could be separated into its two components, making it easier to carry into narrow Chinese apartments.

Furniture manufacturers in countries such as China have developed compact designs with space-saving innovations, such as beds or tables with built-in drawers. By catering to low- and middle-income customers in their home market, Chinese furniture makers have emerged as significant players in the U.S. and other developed markets. Chinese firms have used this experience to begin moving upscale to fine furniture markets, aided by the reduction in U.S. tariff restrictions.

Strategy #4: Streamline Offerings to Make Them More Affordable

With limited budgets, customers will pay only for what they need, so it is important to understand the features that are important to local users and cut the bells and whistles that drive up prices. For example, Tata's Indian Hotels Company launched indiOne in 2004, a chain of low-price hostelries offering single rooms for 900 rupees per night (about $20). This compares with an average nightly room rate of $92 across all the company's hotels, many of them premium properties, and $142 for Hilton hotels worldwide. The new entrant created a category for "smart basic" hotels, providing simple self-service accommodations while offering travelers Wi-Fi Internet connections and flat-screen TVs.

By stripping out costs, Advanced Micro Devices (AMD) created a portable computer for the masses with the launch of its rugged $185 Personal Internet Communicator (including monitor). The product is part of the "50 by 15" initiative, announced by CEO Hector Ruiz, to connect 50 percent of the world's population to the Internet by 2015. AMD created a low-cost chip and a basic design for the shoebox-sized machine. AMD also worked with Microsoft to create a bare-bones operating system for a low price, although it still includes an Explorer browser and a media player that can handle full-screen video feeds. While the profit margins might be a few dollars a machine for AMD, across 100 million machines, this could amount to several hundred million dollars. Targeted users of the new device in rural villages won't even shell out the $185 up front when these machines become available. They are being marketed by local telecom companies, which treat them like cable set-top boxes, including them with an Internet subscription for less than $10 per month.

The costs of technology continue to fall. MIT's Nicholas Negroponte announced a proposal in early 2005 for a $100 laptop for the developing world, using a rear-projection screen and solid-state memory that could be run on batteries or even a hand crank.

Concerns about cost have also helped fuel the spread of open-source software such as Linux. (It is estimated, for example, that Brazil spends more on software licensing fees than on hunger.) Brazil announced plans in 2005 for a program called *PC Conectado* (Connected PC), aimed at helping millions of low-income Brazilians buy their first computers using only free software. Sun Microsystems President Jonathan Schwartz foresees an even cheaper computing system based on UNIX and the Java Desktop System that would be *given away* with a subscription to Internet service.

While products have to be stripped down to their essentials to reduce costs, it is important to recognize that these "essentials" may be different for a particular developing market. For example, a team of researchers at the Indian Institute of Science (IISc) in Bangalore developed the "Simputer," with a price tag of US$200, which has no keyboard, working off a stylus-based text entry system. Yet in some ways it is more powerful than many low-end computers in developed countries. It has a built-in speaker that speaks text entered in Hindi, Kannada, or Tamil. It is powered by three standard batteries, eliminating the need for charging or reliable electrical systems.

Creating low-cost designs for housing can also open the door to growth opportunities. U.S. firm Pulte Homes of Michigan completed about 450,000 homes in Mexico in 2004, along with a group of local developers. These homes are priced around $40,000, and buyers of these homes have an average annual household income of about $14,000 (putting them in the top 30 percent of Mexicans). As a sign of the sector's growth, Mexican builder Homex SA was listed on the New York Stock Exchange in 2004. Major foreign banks such as Citigroup and Spain's Banco Bilbao Vizcaya Argentaria SA are offering attractive mortgages, which is helping fuel the housing boom.

Secondhand products, particularly those imported from the developed world, can also provide low-cost alternatives. The declared value of secondhand clothing exported to Africa surpassed $59 million in 2002. While the transfer of clothing started as a charity, used clothing accounted for 81 percent of garment purchases, according to the Ugandan Manufacturers Association, angering domestic textile makers. Poland became a hot European market for used cars after the nation's entry into the European Union in 2004, when used car imports from other parts of Europe rose to more than 820,000 cars annually.

Strategy #5: Join Many Small Drops to Make an Ocean

When products or services cannot be offered in a modular form or streamlined to reduce costs, companies can use demand pooling to reduce costs to individual users. An entrepreneur in Mexico might buy a 2-liter bottle of Coca-Cola and sell it by the glass outside the back window of a home in the barrio. Or a cell phone lady in Bangladesh might sell cellular service by the call, or companies might offer SMS text messaging by the message. Demand pooling is a way to join many small customers into a larger customer. While developed countries may use demand pooling to purchase group insurance or obtain group discounts, demand pooling is used for much lower-budget items in the developing world. These customers are not just shopping around for a lower price for a particular service, as U.S. insurance customers might be. They can achieve access to the service only through demand pooling.

In rural areas, much of this demand pooling occurs around villages, the natural center of community life. While individual farmers may not be able to afford Internet connections to check on grain prices, several villages full of farmers can. ITC has created the *e-choupal* project (*choupal* means "village square") in India, which places solar battery-powered Internet terminals with satellite access in rural farming villages. These terminals, in the home of a central farmer, serve as a hub for the surrounding farmers. They use the system to discover grain prices, track weather, and find other key information, as well as purchase supplies and sell their products. By 2003, this innovation—launched in 2000 with the help of companies, non-governmental organizations (NGOs), and local governments—had connected 3.1 million farmers through a network of more than 5,000 *e-choupals*, handling $100 million in transactions. ITC adds 30 new villages every day. ITC Chairman Yogesh Chander Deveshwar's ambition is to reach 10 million farmers by 2010 with $2.5 billion in transactions. ITC reports that it recovers its equipment investment from an e-*choupal* in the first year of operation.

In a similar initiative in rural areas, ICICI, India's largest private-sector bank, has established Internet kiosks to provide financial services as well as insurance, education, agriculture, health services, games, Internet access, and e-mail. The bank partners with local entrepreneurs or NGOs. Funds are provided at a relatively low interest rate, but volume makes up for this. Partners understand and help reduce risks, and loans are typically made to groups of 10 women. If one individual defaults, the others are responsible, so they recover the money from the defaulting member. This social network has kept bad debts at a low 1 percent.

While *e-choupal* and ICICI's initiative represent organized demand pooling by creating a network around a central hub, some demand pooling is much more ad hoc. Demand pooling often is done within neighborhoods or among family members. Many of the customers of the warehouse clubs in developing countries are not individuals stocking up their freezers and pantries. Instead, they are informal buying groups, where an extended family or group of friends might purchase larger packages at the warehouse stores and then divide them among themselves. Essentially, the customers create their own informal systems for pooling demand. How can companies cater to these informal buying groups?

Groups of businesses can also join to create a pool of demand. When Peruvian retailer E Wong (discussed in Chapter 3, "Aim for the Ricochet Economy") was founded in 1942, it recognized that initially there was not enough demand to support a large supermarket for individual customers. But it could create a hypermarket for smaller grocers. A grocer might buy a carton of oranges and then resell them individually to its own customers. By serving business customers, and end consumers as the Peruvian retail market developed, E Wong achieved sales of US$576 million through 27 stores in 2003.

Small entrepreneurs also engage in this type of ad hoc demand pooling, such as Indian retailers who offer single cigarettes at small shops. This supports consumers who are engaged in just-in-time consumption. If companies recognize that businesses exist to sell single cigarettes or drinks of soda, how could they better cater to these resellers?

Small Wonders

Given the high populations of developing markets, opportunities exist to make substantial profits on small purchases. A customer might be able to afford only a single sachet of shampoo, a single cigarette, or a 110-pound bag of cement, but many millions of such customers might represent an opportunity. Selling small does add to costs in packaging, distribution, and other areas, so companies need to find ways to keep these costs low. Companies also need to find ways to manage supply chains efficiently through better point-of-sale scanners and accept small payments efficiently. Low-priced scanners and innovations such as payments by mobile phone or debit and credit cards will facilitate this process. As long as every purchase is profitable, these small purchases can add up to super-size profits. After all, remember that McDonald's built a $45 billion global business on meals that cost only a few dollars.

The risks of offering small payments on installments are not as great as developed-world models might indicate. Many of the low-income customers in the developing world are on their way up. They want to preserve their credit. And these risks can be reduced through demand pooling that builds a business around a family, neighborhood, or village. Where can demand be brought together to create viable markets?

While managers may be used to looking at markets with a broad view and targeting only the most profitable segments, this can be a mistake in developing markets. Instead of looking for the very limited segments of the developing world that can afford to buy a company's products as they are currently designed and priced, consider instead how the product and pricing can be reshaped for the market. How can the size be reduced? How can prices be brought down? How can installments be used to bring payments within the reach of potential customers? How can you grow a big business by thinking small?

The 86 Percent Solution

- Identify opportunities for reducing your products' package sizes to reach a broader market. How can you manufacture and distribute them and still make a profit?

- Consider ways to use small installments or subscriptions to reduce the purchase price of products and services.

- Look at the impact of smaller homes and the just-in-time pantry on your products, even for customers who have the resources to make less-frequent bulk purchases. How can you combine several products to conserve space?

- If markets are too poor or small to support purchases of your products, look for ways to pool demand.

Notes

1 Wharton Fellows. India Master Class, March 2005.

2 Peter Menzel. *Material World: A Global Family Portrait*. San Francisco: Sierra Club Books, 1994. Based on United Nations data from the UN International Year of the Family 1994.

7

Bring Your Own
Infrastructure

With unreliable electric grids, undrinkable water, tangled roads, massive informal economies, and other infrastructure gaps in developing markets, companies often need to creatively build or bring their own infrastructure.

An itinerant photographer, Seha stops in at a small kahvehane, *or coffeehouse, in a village in rural Turkey. He offers to take a digital photo of the shop owner and his family for 1 new Turkish lira, or about 70 cents. He barters part of the price of his coffee. The Hewlett-Packard camera and small printer are both battery-powered, and Seha can recharge them with a solar charger that he carries in his backpack. Except for occasional trips to Ankara to restock the paper and ink for his printer, he is a fairly self-sufficient entrepreneur who makes a good business traveling from village to village recording the milestones of weddings or births, or taking a first family photo.*

Even without the disruptions of earthquakes or other disasters, electricity in the rural areas is unpredictable and sometimes nonexistent. In a larger village, Seha stops at a kiosk, where he checks his e-mail for a small fee. The computer runs on a noisy gasoline-powered generator, which makes it hard to concentrate, and the narrow streets are very crowded. Seha also carries a small water purification system because of the uncertain local water supplies. In larger towns, he sometimes sends money to his mother, Esra, back in his home village through a money-transfer service. Seha smiles as he walks down the dusty road, thankful that he can carry his infrastructure with him. He is relatively independent due to the income of his small business and his ability to exist apart from an uncertain infrastructure. And, of course, none of his income is reported to the government. To the formal economy, he is virtually invisible. He is very glad to be living off the grid.

Even a small entrepreneur such as Seha cannot assume there will be infrastructure to support him. How can you work around holes in the environment of developing markets or find opportunities in filling infrastructure gaps?

The maglev train in Shanghai is a marvel, a sleek transportation system that floats on a magnetic cushion without the rumbles and shakes of traditional trains. Yet the train, launched in January 2004, is also an example of the complexities of infrastructure in emerging markets. On the trip to the airport, it takes a 20-minute cab ride along streets crowded with bicycles from the skyscrapers of the Pudong section of Shanghai to reach the maglev train's terminal. Once there, passengers enjoy a breathtaking 8-minute ride at speeds of up to 432 kilometers per hour (268 miles per hour), almost twice the rate of the fastest trains on the heavily traveled Northeast corridor in the U.S. The terminal on the other side offers another harsh dose of reality, with a 5-minute hike to the Pudong International Airport. Like much of the infrastructure of the developing world, this lightning-fast trip is a shining island of the future surrounded by crumbling systems of the past.

Developing countries have patches of infrastructure that are stellar, better than anywhere in the world, but all this new infrastructure has been built quickly and often rests on a shaky and unreliable foundation. It is like building a supersonic jet while it is flying. Fast or slow, it is inevitably a wild ride. Weaknesses in infrastructure demand different approaches from companies that operate in developing markets and also present opportunities for innovators who can fill the gaps.

A Tale of Two Markets

Across the developing world, the World Bank estimated in 2003 that a fifth of the population does not have access to clean water and sanitation facilities, about half live on less than $2 per day, and a quarter of adults are illiterate.[1] An estimated 32 percent do not have access to electricity. Yet these same countries have some of the most rapid rates of adoption for cell phones, computers, automobiles, and other products. While perhaps one million Indians may work in air-conditioned office buildings of information technology (IT) services companies in Bangalore, the surrounding countryside lacks basic services.

Although there are extreme differences in the level and quality of infrastructure, it is important to recognize that the impact of infrastructure weaknesses is not just in poor, rural segments. Everyone in India rides on the pothole-filled Grand Trunk Road that leads from Delhi to Agra, where the Taj Mahal is located. It is filled with cars, trucks, and bullock carts. Roads often are poor or nonexistent, telephone networks are often down, and electricity is uncertain. There is a shortage of potable water and good sanitation, and water shortages are expected to become more severe with economic growth and the expansion of irrigated agriculture. According to U.S. government estimates, per-capita water availability in India is likely to drop by 50 to 75 percent between 2000 and 2015. Levels of pollution and noise are rising. Countries such as India and China have started massive projects to build seaports and airports, creating opportunities for construction companies. Many of the railway and road systems are a century old (or more) and are in desperate need of upgrades.

Rapid development itself has placed added strains on the systems of these developing countries. China's streets are so jammed with automobiles that Shanghai proposed banning bicycles in part of the city. India's Karnataka state, where the booming high-tech capital of Bangalore is located, has swelled to almost twice the population of California with only a tenth of the power-generation capacity. China's infrastructure is straining under the weight of its double-digit growth rates. In mid-2004, 24 of China's 31 provinces and major municipalities were experiencing shortages of electricity. Demand for coal for power generation has led to a "coal famine" in China. Factories facing prolonged blackouts and brownouts during peak periods set up their own generation systems and closed for weeklong "high-temperature holidays." By 2004, China's generating capacity was about 30 gigawatts short of what it needed, a shortfall roughly equivalent to the entire capacity of a country such as Turkey or Norway. A Liz Claiborne factory in China hired one employee whose sole job was to look after vital diesel fuel.

Population growth and rapid urbanization are straining water systems in Malaysia. With brown water flowing from the taps in Kuala Lumpur, the government announced a 50 billion Malaysian ringgits (US$13.2 billion) overhaul of its water and sewer services over the next five years. Also, traffic, construction, and generators are creating rising noise pollution. (Two-thirds of the 250 million people who have disabling hearing impairment live in developing countries.) While companies are working to make quieter cars and washing machines for developed markets, who is addressing the growing noise pollution of the developing world?

Trash is a major problem in the developing world. The UN estimates that only between 25 and 55 percent of all waste in large cities is collected by municipal authorities. More than 5 million people die each year from diseases related to inadequate waste disposal systems.[2]

Total water and sanitation coverage is absent from many parts of the world, as shown in Table 7-1. Even in countries with relatively high average coverage of water and sanitation, rural areas are often left behind. For example, while total Mexican sanitation coverage was at 73 percent in 2000, rural coverage was just 32 percent. In addition to the direct impact, sanitation shortages also have indirect effects as young women drop out of school or experience stomach problems as a result of the lack of sanitation facilities. (Because of the lack of privacy, they are forced to wait until before sunrise or after sunset to relieve themselves.)

TABLE 7-1   Water and Sanitation Coverage (2000)

Country	Percentage of Total Water Supply Coverage	Percentage of Total Sanitation Coverage
Afghanistan	13%	12%
Angola	38%	44%
Bangladesh	97%	53%
China	75%	38%
Ecuador	71%	59%
Ethiopia	24%	15%
Haiti	46%	28%
India	88%	31%
Nepal	81%	27%
Niger	59%	20%
Mexico	86%	73%

Source: World Health Organization, Global Water Supply and Sanitation Assessment, 2000 Report

The impact of infrastructure weaknesses in developing markets was dramatically illustrated in early 2005 by the death of Prime Minister Zurab Zhvania in the former Soviet nation of Georgia. He died of carbon monoxide poisoning after a space heater in the apartment of a political acquaintance malfunctioned. In a country where central heating is rare, this was not an unusual event. Georgia saw 45 other deaths from carbon monoxide in the preceding three years.

Regulatory and Financial Infrastructure

Weaknesses in infrastructure extend beyond the physical grids to the less-tangible gaps in regulations or economic systems that create breeding grounds for thriving informal economies. A World Bank study estimates that the informal or parallel economy generates more than 40 percent of the GNP of developing countries, compared to 18 percent of the GNP of developed countries. In Zimbabwe, the figure is as high as 60 percent. Informal markets account for $20 billion in sales in the information technology sector alone and as much as 50 percent of sales of health and beauty aids in some countries. In Brazil, where the informal economy accounts for an estimated 40 percent of gross national income, a study concluded that tighter government controls could help the economy grow by an additional 1.5 percent per year. Indian sales of shadow-market computers outnumber legitimate sales by two to one and account for 70 percent of Malaysian cell phone sales. By 2004, given many exceptions such as agricultural income, only about 3 percent of India's total population paid income tax. The informal economy accounts for an estimated 80 percent of employment in sub-Saharan Africa and 70 percent in India, Indonesia, Pakistan, and the Philippines. A study in the Philippines estimated that the country loses $8 billion a year due to tax evasion.

Copying and stealing products is widespread. The World Customs Organization estimates that 7 percent of world merchandise, or more than $500 billion worth of goods in 2004, is from counterfeit products, with about two-thirds coming from China. Rampant cable TV piracy in Asia, particularly in India and Thailand, cost the industry nearly US$1 billion in 2004, and Brazilian cable pirates have set up an estimated 600,000 illicit cable connections. Intellectual property is also very fluid, although protections are improving. A study of World Health Organization data found that only 1.4 percent of "essential" medicines are protected by patents in developing countries. GM Daewoo filed a lawsuit against Chinese automaker Chery in 2004, alleging that the company copied design and technologies from a GM Daewoo car for Chery's QQ model. It is one of several intellectual property suits against Chinese carmakers.

As economies develop, the legal and financial infrastructure generally strengthens. For example, rising outside investment in Korean businesses has led to regulatory reforms that have weakened the tight control of traditional *chaebols* (business groups). A 2004 McKinsey study found, however, that the informal economy is growing in many countries, despite development.

Finding Opportunities in Infrastructure

Managers cannot wait for governments to solve these infrastructure problems. Companies need to either bring their own infrastructure or innovate around the limitations. The motto should be "Don't wait; innovate." These solutions can lead to highly profitable businesses. While infrastructure weaknesses present challenges for businesses, weak infrastructures also create opportunities for companies that can sell products or solutions to fill in these gaps on a local level—such as local generators or water filtration systems. Companies also can develop creative work-around solutions that avoid these gaps in the infrastructure altogether—such as low-water detergents, solar-powered devices, and ready-to-eat foods that don't require refrigeration. Each weakness in the infrastructure has a silver lining of opportunity, as shown in Table 7-2.

TABLE 7-2   How Infrastructure Weaknesses Create Opportunities

Weakness	Opportunities
Lack of refrigeration	Ready-to-eat meals that don't require refrigeration
Lack of reliable electricity	Generator sets (gensets) and generators
High noise	Noise-reducing appliances and other devices
Poor trash collection	Transform discarded waste into recycled products or fuel
Lack of potable drinking water	Water filters and bottled water
Water shortages	Low-water detergents, waterless razors
Poor highways and road systems	Vehicles designed for these conditions
Lack of resources for travelers	Organized car rental companies and hotels
Financial and regulatory infrastructure, shadow economy	Legitimate businesses to meet the needs of the shadow economy

Strategy #1: Create Markets in the Gaps

Businesses that can find ways to fill in the gaps in the infrastructure for consumers can find significant opportunities in the developing world. Companies have developed domestic gensets (generator sets) and inverters (backup, battery-like power sources) to provide purchasers with an unbroken power supply. Entrepreneurs are setting up gensets in urban areas with poor power supplies and selling electricity at multiples of the regular rates. Cummins Power, which had been the leading maker of large generators in India, created customizable gensets that grew to 25 percent of its revenue in India by 2004. It is building on its successes there to export these generators to Africa, Latin America, and the Middle East. The small generators can be customized to specific applications (such as noise reduction for hospitals), or several can be wired together to meet larger generation needs. Honda has also developed efficient, super-quiet inverter generators, some of which produce no more noise than inside the average private office.

Similarly, clean water is a problem in many developing countries, but this has created a market for portable water purification systems and bottled water. In India, local brands such as Aquagard water filters and Bisleri bottled water were so successful that they led the way for multinational companies to launch their own brands. The success of Femsa bottled water in the 1990s in Mexico encouraged Coca-Cola to launch its Ciel brand of water in 1997. Growth of water sales in emerging markets is significantly higher than in other markets because of the poor quality of local tap water and because a ready supply of bottled water helps tourism (ending jokes by tourists that "You can't drink the water.") Procter & Gamble created Pur, a powder that could be added to contaminated water to purify it for drinking (which it donated to relief efforts after the tsunami in South Asia in December 2004).

Many other aspects of physical and economic infrastructure can create opportunities for companies. These include transportation services such as rental cars, overnight accommodations, insurance, and banking services. Gaps in these and other areas of the infrastructure create opportunities for companies that can fill them. These services have their own distinctive twists in developing markets. For example, rental cars usually come with drivers in these countries, so there are different sets of logistical challenges in managing not only a fleet of cars but also a staff of drivers.

Sulabh International Social Service Organization, founded by Dr. Bindeshwar Pathak in India, has helped fill the sanitation gap by creating low-cost toilets. They conserve water and are specifically designed for the 2.4 billion people in the world, including 700 million in India, who either have no organized system of sanitation or have only unhygienic facilities.[3] In addition to building the only "toilet museum" in the world, Sulabh has built 3,200 community toilets with bath, laundry, and toilet facilities operated on a pay-and-use basis, serving more than 10 million people and employing 50,000 workers. (This is still just a small fraction of the need.) Although Sulabh is a charitable organization, these facilities are designed to be self-sufficient based on income from those who use them. Is it a great leap to consider that there might be an opportunity for a profitable business? It may not be as glamorous as cell phones and Internet service, but when you have a true unmet market need affecting more than 2 billion people, doesn't that sound like an opportunity? (This issue is getting more attention globally with the work of international organizations such as the World Toilet Organization—the other WTO—which holds an annual international summit.)

Sometimes infrastructure solutions require a deep understanding of the nature of consumer behavior. Amil Assistencia Medica Internacional, one of Brazil's largest health-care companies, was trying to determine why women from the ghettos of Rio de Janeiro were not taking advantage of government-sponsored medical care. In interviews, they found that transportation to the medical centers and child care were the biggest obstacles. The company set up a free bus service that allowed women to come and bring their small children. By filling in these missing pieces of the infrastructure, it was able to encourage women to take advantage of health-care services.

In addition to addressing the physical infrastructure, companies are using creative approaches to fill gaps in the financial infrastructure. While people in developing countries are underbanked, high cell phone penetration is creating a market for online credit card transactions where there are no banks or land lines. Visa International, for example, is working closely with governments and lenders in developing markets to design wireless banking and credit card systems. Debit and credit card holders in China surpassed 700 million by 2005 (primarily debit cards). HSBC Holdings partnered with the Bank of Shanghai and the Bank of Communications, Citigroup joined with Pudong Development Bank, and American Express joined with Industrial and Commercial Bank of China to offer cards. (A domestic partner is required by regulation until further deregulation in 2006.) Collaborating with Visa Mobile, China's largest cell phone companies are offering customers systems for paying bills and making small purchases through bank accounts and credit cards, helping accelerate the shift to digital finance in a market with more than 300 million mobile phones but only a few million credit cards.

Strategy #2: Create Work-Around Solutions

While an acute shortage of water in rural villages in India would appear to be a tremendous obstacle for a company selling laundry detergent, Hindustan Lever saw it as an opportunity. Many Indians do not have access to running water, and others have access for only a few hours per day. The shortage of water in some parts of India is so acute that it has even impacted the purchase and use of washing machines, which require significantly more water than traditional hand washing.

Hindustan Lever reformulated and relaunched its Surf Excel brand in the middle of 2003 with a "low suds" formula that cut water consumption in half. While Surf originally had been positioned to emphasize "stain removal," its new positioning was "outstanding stain removal with half the water, effort, or time." In addition to meeting the need for water conservation, the new product also tapped into a growing desire for convenience by reducing the effort spent on household chores. As scarcity of water becomes an increasingly important issue around the globe, this product could find potential in many other markets. Gillette launched a very successful razor in India that was designed to be cleaned without running water.

In 1996, London-based Freeplay developed a radio for the African market to overcome the lack of an electrical infrastructure. The radio was powered by cranking a handle, avoiding the need for expensive batteries, and bringing news, agricultural broadcasts, and school lessons to poor and rural listeners. Freeplay has sold more than 3 million radios (also selling them in the West, where they turned out to be popular with campers). The company also sells hand-powered flashlights and medical equipment.

Given the lack of reliable electricity and refrigeration, food companies have been very successful in developing ready-to-eat meals that don't require refrigeration. In India, MTR Foods Ltd. has introduced a variety of instant food mixes (including burfi mix, a sweet) that take just 15 minutes to prepare. These foods take advantage of a growing demand for easy-to-prepare foods driven by an increasing number of women in the workforce. MTR had a goal of reaching sales of 5 billion rupees (US$110 million) by 2005. Around the globe, shelf-stable ready-to-eat meals have grown by more than 6 percent per year in recent years with solid growth in emerging markets, Asia Pacific, and North America.

Companies can sometimes overcome weaknesses in infrastructure through product design. For example, chocolates typically need to be stored at 18 to 20 degrees Celsius. This is often not possible in India, where cooling can be erratic and summer temperatures soar above 45 degrees Celsius. At these high temperatures, the fat in the chocolate oozes out and forms a white coating. To avoid this, the chocolates are designed with a much lower fat content that allows them to be stable at up to 30 to 32 degrees Celsius. Shop owners sometimes store the chocolates in the summer in coolers provided by soft drink companies, but sales still drop in the summer, when chocolates tend to get sticky.

Strategy #3: Find Treasure in Trash

The saying that "One man's trash is another man's treasure" is certainly true in developing countries. China's voracious demand for recyclable paper for packaging and other uses in its growing economy has driven up prices for waste paper in neighboring Japan. Demand and prices are so high that Tokyo businesses are hiring security guards to stop roving "apaches" from poaching their recycling bins.

In Kenya, Chardust Ltd., an alternative energy company head-quartered on the outskirts of Nairobi, has developed innovative techniques to convert biomass wastes into low-cost charcoal briquettes. They sell over 180 tons per month to institutional and domestic markets in Kenya, displacing an equivalent amount of unsustainably harvested lumpwood charcoal. While providing a cheaper energy alternative, this contributes to job creation, waste recycling, and environmental conservation. The company also manufactures heaters to burn the briquettes. Similarly, biogas generators can convert garbage into power for lights and water pumps, addressing the shortage of energy and the overabundance of garbage and other waste in one solution. These generators also avoid the noise pollution that comes from noisy fossil-fuel generators.

Cemex has designed equipment to use petroleum coke, a discarded byproduct of oil refineries, and even oily rags and old tires to run its kilns in Mexico, cutting its energy bills by 17 percent. It even sells leftover power to the public utility. Other companies in areas with costly and unreliable energy, such as India and Brazil, have developed more efficient processes and have adapted to use cheaper fuels or hydroelectric power.

Sometimes the infrastructure demands in one part of growing economies (demand for paper or power, for example) can be met by utilizing discards (paper trash or biomass) from their own market or from neighbors. In meeting the infrastructure demands through such approaches, other pressing problems such as a growing trash crisis, with its negative impact on health and sanitation, can be addressed at the same time.

Strategy #4: Build the Infrastructure to Support the Business

In addition to building infrastructure for others, companies need to look at their own supply chains and systems to ensure that they have the right infrastructure to support their businesses. At each step along the value chain from the company to customers, managers need to look for ways to fill the missing infrastructure. For example, Coca-Cola in Brazil uses ice boxes to keep its product cold in small villages with erratic power supplies or no power. In towns with more reliable power supplies, family fridges, appliances that are shared by several families, keep the product cold. Soft drink companies are also experimenting with eutectic coolers, which are specially designed for areas that experience frequent long power outages. These coolers have a built-in jacket with a eutectic cooling solution, which is cooled when power is running. They hold the temperature for up to 10 hours without power. These coolers also eliminate the use of an air-cooled condenser and fan motor, reducing energy consumption. Electrolux Kelvinator developed a refrigerator for the Indian market that can keep ice cold even after a six-hour power failure. Nokia's most popular Indian cell phone includes a built-in flashlight and a dust-resistant keypad.

To keep its Brazilian vending machines running, Coca-Cola has established its own local service infrastructure to ensure lower repair and maintenance costs. The company has created vending machines to perform under conditions of up to 75 percent humidity and temperatures of up to 105 degrees Fahrenheit (40.5 Celsius). Because most Brazilian retail shops are not air-conditioned, the air drafts in the soda cooling system are designed to prevent condensation on the glass doors from the hot, humid air from coming into contact with cold surfaces.

When companies launch new businesses or plants in developing countries, they often have to build the supporting infrastructure at the same time. When KenCall set up its African call center in Kenya, it needed to use a costly satellite hookup to bypass the country's terrible phone system. It also needed to build a backup generator system to keep its computers running through frequent power failures. Companies such as McDonald's have set up local suppliers of potatoes, meat, and other products to ensure that the local restaurants have the right inputs and to maintain consistent quality across all their outlets. Car companies such as Tata Motors in India have created their own local parts and service networks to support their sales. Sometimes companies have to look abroad to find the right inputs for the businesses. To meet a demand for aluminum and iron ore, China's state-owned Minmetals made a $5 billion acquisition of Canadian mining giant Noranda in 2004, the first such deal of its magnitude.

Tremendous opportunities exist for companies that can overcome infrastructure weaknesses. UK steelmaker Mittal Steel, founded by Calcutta-born industrialist Lakshmi Mittal, has become the largest, most geographically diverse steel company in the world by focusing on underappreciated assets in the developing world, often poorly run state-owned industries. Mittal started from a small operation in India and expanded by recognizing opportunities for acquisitions and turnarounds in countries such as Indonesia, Kazakhstan, Mexico, and Trinidad and Tobago. Finally, it expanded into the U.S. and the UK. The reason Mittal can find value in these underutilized assets is that he has perfected a system for installing strong management and creating his own infrastructure to support the steel operations. With $7 billion in annual operating income, Mittal owns a network of mills in 14 countries, producing 57 million tons of metal annually. He has become the third-richest man in the world.

Strategy #5: Use Existing Infrastructure Creatively

NIIT became India's largest IT trainer under the chairmanship of Rajendra S. Pawar by creating a chain of training centers across the country. It needed a different model when it entered China in 1998. The Chinese government required a joint venture with a local company. NIIT had a tough time initially, until it realized it could partner with an existing network of local universities. By changing its business model to take advantage of this existing infrastructure of university campuses, NIIT created more than 100 education centers on the campuses of 10 leading universities, allowing it to cover 80 percent of China's provinces by 2004. Building on its successes in China, the company moved to other Asia-Pacific markets, such as Thailand, Malaysia, Indonesia, and the Philippines, to become Asia's largest IT trainer. NIIT also found creative ways to connect with the best and brightest Indian youth through its support of chess programs in schools. In 1999, NIIT named Viswanathan Anand, one of the world's best chess masters, its brand ambassador. Anand visits schools across India and gives advice on the Internet, serving as a role model and helping the company connect with promising young students for its IT education programs.

A New Ballgame

To establish the Friendship Basketball League, aspiring to become the Chinese NCAA, U.S. promoter Leonard Bloom had to build a university infrastructure virtually from scratch. He provided universities with rule books, exercise plans, red-and-yellow basketballs, uniforms, and team names. By the league's launch, he had invested more than $1 million in the infrastructure. He hoped to regain these costs through media rights and a contract to act as exclusive agent of all the players in the league for five years after they graduate.

Strategy #6: Look for Opportunities in the Shadows

The shadow economy can point to opportunities that might be met through more legitimate channels if pricing and regulation change—or can be changed. For example, at a time when lipsticks and cosmetics were viewed as signs of personal vanity and bourgeois values by Communist leaders in Vietnam, they had to be smuggled in from China. But with the liberalization of Vietnamese markets, South Korean company LG Corp. moved quickly to build its cosmetics brand De Bon. De Bon became the top-selling cosmetics brand and, aided by Korean television shows, it helped shape the definition of beauty for a generation of Vietnamese women. A shadow business during times of restrictions had become a booming legitimate industry.

Sometimes companies can bring informal or shadow operators into their legitimate businesses. Global drug manufacturers have some-times slowed or stopped unauthorized generic copies of their drugs that are going off patent by penning early deals with local drugmakers to create authorized generics. For example, GlaxoSmithKline PLC ended legal action against India's Par Pharmaceutical Cos. over its anti-depressant Paxil by signing Par to distribute an authorized generic ver-sion of the drug. The illegitimate channel is made legitimate.

China is notorious for having perhaps the largest music piracy market in the world (with some 95 percent of all songs pirated at an estimated value of $600 million). However, it is important to remember that it also has the second-biggest *legitimate* music mar-ket in Asia, estimated at more than $100 million. The legal market has seen double-digit growth every year since China joined the World Trade Organization (WTO) in 2001. Companies such as TimeWarner are using strategies of rapid release of legal videos and DVDs to reduce piracy, bringing out the home versions just days after theatrical releases.

Shadow markets can also expand the overall market size rather than cannibalizing existing markets. For example, a survey of managers of health-and-beauty-aid companies concluded that 25 percent of gray-market sales were not in competition with authorized distributors. In other words, they extended the market. And once customers come in through the shadow market, companies can sometimes sell them more advanced services and equipment. (This is similar to how software makers offer users free trials and basic versions of digital music players or antivirus software before asking them to trade up to the premium versions.)

Shadow markets can also help build the critical mass so that legitimate producers can achieve economies of scope and scale. This means that intellectual property theft can sometimes be positive for the "victim." NewCorp.'s Rupert Murdoch recognized this when he called the Asian pirates who stole the signals from his Star TV satellite system and resold it over cable "splendid entrepreneurs." While Star may be missing out on some revenue, these pirates are helping broaden the company's market, and this penetration allows the company to raise its advertising rates. Similarly, computer software companies could add advertising, offers for upgrades, or product placements to generate revenue from the broader user base created by piracy.

Often the informal economy uses work-around solutions that point to the need for legitimate business solutions. For example, the financial system known as *hawala* transfers cash funds internationally through informal, off-the-books networks. The substantial flows through such informal systems pointed to the need for a cheaper alternative to very expensive wire transfers offered by banks. As discussed in Chapter 3, "Aim for the Ricochet Economy," many companies have stepped into this gap to offer legitimate, low-cost, person-to-person international transfers at much lower costs than banks.

Strategy #7: Recognize Unseen Rivals, and Build Barriers to Keep Them Out

Invisible competitors in the informal economy can compete directly with the formal economy, but without the constraints of regulation, taxation, or branding. For example, when one Latin American country opened its markets to foreign oil companies in the mid-1990s, small entrepreneurial firms began rebottling domestic automobile oil in the branded containers of U.S. companies, selling them at higher prices to take advantage of their brand reputations. This informal economy accounted for a large part of the oil sold in the country, angering both the foreign companies and the state oil company. These companies could have taken steps to thwart such piracy through marketing and education or tighter control of distribution channels.

Aggressive pricing can sometimes deflect attacks from shadow firms. With pirated software accounting for an estimated 89 percent of software in Russia and 70 percent in India, Microsoft launched a "Windows Lite" operating system in developing countries in 2004 at a fraction of its standard price.

Companies can also create profitable businesses by designing systems that make it harder for the shadow economy to operate. When trucking companies in Pakistan were facing rampant corruption in gas and oil purchases—with cash-paying drivers accepting kickbacks from corrupt operators at the pump—shifting to prepaid cards and credit cards helped control this behavior. Using this strategy, Pakistan Oil Company built a successful business by helping companies better track and control their expenses and limit their exposure to employee theft.

Quality guarantees are another way to shine light on the shadows. In India, where close to 80 percent of jewelry has a lower karatage than advertised, Tanishq has become the leading jeweler by bringing discipline to the sector. It certified the purity of its gold and even offered a "19k = 22k" exchange in 2004 that allowed owners of "impure" jewelry of at least 19k to receive a 22k gold replacement for no additional cost. Tanishq is turning the defects and shadows of the market into a "golden" opportunity, helping organize the entire sector. Sometimes technology can also help restore consumer trust in sectors where it has been eroded. For example, when STD pay phones were initially installed in small stores throughout India, assessing charges was left to local shopkeepers. When a readout was installed to show time and costs, making charges more transparent to customers, usage increased significantly.

Strategy #8: Ride Up the Supply Chain and into Developed Markets

Developing market companies can build their own distribution channels to increase their share of profits. Colombian farmers, for example, who typically receive about 1 percent of the $3 cost of a cappuccino in a developed-world café, launched their own chain of cafés. Building on

Juan Valdez coffee

a character and logo that had been established as the symbol of 100% Colombian coffee more than two decades ago, the National Federation of Coffee Growers of Colombia set up a chain of Juan Valdez coffee shops. The first opened in Colombia in December 2003, giving growers a larger share of the profits from sales. Federation plans called for up to 300 branches worldwide by 2007, including at least eight shops in the U.S. (one in Seattle, in Starbucks' backyard). By expanding their infrastructure and strong branding, Colombian coffee growers have been able to improve their returns and move into the developed world.

In India, CEO Sunil Mittal of the Bharti Group joined with de Rothschilds of Europe to launch the FieldFresh brand, which will take the fresh vegetables of rural Indian farmers to markets in Asia, the Middle East, and central Asian countries. This initiative and others are improving productivity by modernizing farming while offering greater returns through processing or branding.

Overlapping Infrastructures

In the absence of a strong central infrastructure, one of the characteristics of emerging markets is a complex set of overlapping infrastructures. In addition to public infrastructure for electricity, water, sanitation, trash collection, and other basic services, a private-sector infrastructure is designed to fill in the gaps. Pieces of infrastructure are supplied by nongovernmental organizations (NGOs) and a variety of nonprofit organizations. The submerged infrastructure of the shadow economy is also a factor.

These overlapping infrastructures are the reality of emerging markets. The various layers of infrastructure can help support businesses and create channels to customers. Where gaps exist, companies have opportunities to fill them or develop creative work-arounds. As discussed in the next chapter, sometimes these gaps also turn out to have a silver lining—an opportunity to leapfrog—as with the rapid spread of cellular service in the developing world, thanks to freedom from the burden of legacy land lines.

The 86 Percent Solution

- Identify the gaps in infrastructure in the markets you are in or are planning to enter. For each gap, look for an opportunity that is created. If there is a water shortage, for example, how can you redesign your products to use less water? If there is a shortage of reliable electricity, how can you help meet this need?

- For each gap in the infrastructure, look at how it will affect your business operations. Think of ways you can create work-around solutions to fill in the holes.

- Consider ways you can turn "trash" into "treasure" by recycling an infrastructure problem into a solution.

- Examine ways you can use different technologies and approaches to create a substitute infrastructure.

- Look at the opportunities and threats created by the informal economy. How could they hurt your business? What market opportunities do they indicate that could be met through legitimate channels?

- Look at moving up the supply chain. Are there opportunities to move into other parts of the chain to expand your business?

Notes

1 *Partnerships in Development*, The World Bank Group, 2004.

2 United Nations Center for Human Settlements, United Nations Development Program, cited at the Global Development Research Center. "Key Facts on Waste Issues." http://www.gdrc.org/uem/waste/key-facts.html.

3 Bindeshwar Pathak. "Sulabh Sanitation Technologies to Achieve Millennium Development Goals on Sanitation." Delhi Sustainable Development Summit 2004.

8

LOOK FOR THE
LEAPFROG

Lack of infrastructure can sometimes represent a greenfield opportunity that allows 86 percent markets to find opportunities by leapfrogging forward to more advanced technological solutions.

Mikhail leans forward in his chair in the living room of his Moscow apartment. He clicks the mouse on his new computer, running Windows XP Starter edition, which cost less than 1,000 rubles (US$36). The computer also plays CDs and television shows, so he has eliminated the need to buy a CD player and flat-screen television. And he no longer has to use the free computers in the local library or other public areas, where many of his fellow citizens are leaping across the so-called "digital divide."

Mikhail sends an e-mail to a friend about a plan they have to start an online export business. Mikhail doesn't have much experience in business, but he has been learning quickly. He has tapped into a large global network of business books in digital libraries that he is reading online, and he has learned a lot from entrepreneurial sites at the Indian School of Business, the Wharton School, and the University of Texas. He has even called up an online syllabus from an MBA entrepreneurial management course at the Wharton School and has ordered some of the books from the local library.

As he passes through Red Square on the bus to work, Mikhail text-messages his girlfriend, Natasha, on his VimpelCom cell phone about plans for that evening. Since he moved to his new apartment, the mobile phone has been his only phone. He didn't want to go through the costs, red tape, and long wait to get a land line, so he joined the rapidly growing group of wireless users in the city. Only about 1 percent of the Russian population owned a cell phone in 1999, but just five years later, 90 percent of the residents of Moscow and St. Petersburg were toting cell phones—and Mikhail was one of them. A low-cost phone, packaged with a prepaid card, meant that he didn't even need to go through the red tape of going to a bank for a credit card to own his own phone.

The bus moves past the tall spires of St. Basil's cathedral, symbol of the nation's rich traditions, but Mikhail now feels that he is moving rapidly into the future. For consumers such as Mikhail, digital books, computers, mobile phones (and other innovations such as satellite connections and solar panels, which provide communications and electricity to rural areas) are allowing developing countries to leapfrog into the future. How can you look for opportunities to leapfrog with them?

Just as some gaps in the infrastructure create opportunities for companies that can fill them (as discussed in Chapter 7, "Bring Your Own Infrastructure"), other gaps create the opportunity to leap forward to next-generation technologies. As illustrated in Table 8-1, weaknesses in the current infrastructure of developing nations create a variety of leapfrog opportunities. Instead of laying telephone land lines, developing countries have moved directly to cellular. Instead of building large power plants and electrical distribution grids, they are looking at advanced solar power or small nuclear plants. Instead of using physical libraries and schools, they are creating digital ones. The adoption of such technology is surprisingly rapid among citizens hungry to move into a more developed life and make connections with the world.

TABLE 8-1   Leapfrog Opportunities

Weakness	Opportunity to Leapfrog
Poor land-line communications	Cellular, satellite, and voice-over-IP
Lack of reliable electric grids	Solar, plant-based energy sources; small-scale nuclear
Poor distribution infrastructure	Digitize
Lack of education	E-learning
Poor health care	Biosciences, telehealth
Environmental problems	Shift to electric and natural-gas cars

The developing world has few legacy systems. This seems to be a weakness, but as any company that has wrestled to adapt its legacy systems can testify, not being burdened by the past has its advantages:

- Systems can be built from the ground up using the latest technology, and they can be designed for optimal performance.

- Old systems have no sunk costs to amortize. There are no switching costs for customers to move to the new system.

- Adoption rates tend to be extremely high because of pent-up demand, government support, and the momentum of a rapid build-up.

Governments and companies also fuel the spread of technologies. Political leaders are making large investments in creating the infrastructure for technologies that are seen as crucial in economic progress. Companies are encouraging the spread of these technologies through business models based on leapfrog technologies. Cell phones, computers, and broadband Internet access open the way to other innovations.

Leapfrog Strategies

The rapid spread of new technologies in the developing world creates a set of opportunities for companies that can take advantage of the leapfrogging or use technological innovation to create their own opportunities.

Strategy #1: Ride the Waves of Rapid Adoption

Technology spreads very rapidly in developing countries, creating huge opportunities for companies that can ride these waves of adoption. By the end of 2004, developing countries had surpassed developed countries in share of the world's cell phones. India and China had more cell phone subscribers than land-line users. This is a rich source of opportunity for companies that can overcome the challenges of serving developing countries. For example, Egyptian entrepreneur Naguib Sawiris built Orascom into a $2 billion cell phone empire by serving neglected developing countries such as Iraq, Algeria, Bangladesh, and Pakistan. By 2005, the company had 14 million subscribers in nine countries.

Mobile phones are not just for talking. Customers in the developing world are also rapidly adopting diverse services on these phones, seeing them as a "remote control for life." The rise of mobile phones in India has built the fortunes of companies such as Reliance and the

Bhariti Group, led by Sunil Mittal. Reliance, led by the Ambani family, has attracted more than 10,000 registered developers who are creating web service programs for its phones. Companies are developing abbreviated entertainment such as "micro-lit" stories and phone soap operas designed for this medium. The late Dhirubhai Ambani, founder of Reliance, expressed a vision that when cellular phone service becomes cheaper than a stamp, a phone could be a substitute for the postal system.

Other technologies are also spreading rapidly. Internet use in developing countries such as China, India, Brazil, and Mexico grew more rapidly than in the U.S. from 2000 to 2005, as shown in Figure 8-1. By 2010, there are expected to be more than a billion computer users worldwide, up from about 660 million in 2004, primarily as a result of new adopters in China, Russia, India, and other parts of the developing world.

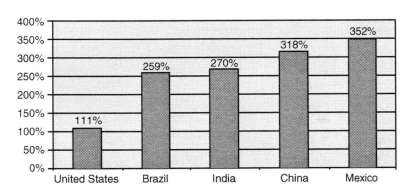

FIGURE 8-1   Growth in Internet users from 2000 to 2005. (Source: Internet World Stats, http://www.internetworldstats.com/stats2.htm#north)

Lenovo, founded by Chuanzhi Liu, has emerged as a global player by riding the rapid spread of computing technology. Foreign firms such as Dell also have experienced rapid growth in developing markets. By 2003, China had become Intel's third-largest market in the world, generating $3.7 billion in revenue, about half the size of Intel's entire U.S. business ($7.4 billion).

While most U.S. users access the Internet through dial-up services, developing-market users, with government help and highly concentrated populations in the cities, are going directly to broadband. While only 6 percent of Chile's population had Internet connections in 2004, more than half of these were high-speed broadband. The future might be seen in South Korea. As it has rapidly developed, it has surged past the U.S. in broadband access. Only about 20 percent of U.S. households had broadband connections in 2004, but three-quarters of Korean households had always-on, high-speed Internet connections. And Korean access speeds are faster than the connections available to most American businesses.

It is not just the high-end urban markets that are adopting these technologies. ITC's e-choupal initiative has gathered rural Indian farmers around satellite-connected hubs, where they can check grain prices (as discussed in Chapter 6, "Grow Big by Thinking Small"). Indian fishermen are using cell phones to price their catches, and auto-rickshaw drivers are carrying cell phones to communicate with customers.

Strategy #2: Digitize

While e-books and other digital media are a bit of a novelty in the developed world, they are something different altogether in the developing world. In developed markets, e-books might represent another channel for books that are readily available from libraries or bookstores. In the developing world, these books are likely to open up whole avenues of knowledge to readers who have no other access to this information.

For example, the Indian School of Business (ISB) in Hyderabad has created a digital library of classic business books such as Adam Smith's *The Wealth of Nations*, as well as online journals, to provide free, "anytime, anywhere" access to information. The Million Book Digital Library Project spearheaded by Professor Raj Reddy at

Carnegie Mellon University is working on an initiative to offer a free-to-read, searchable library of one million books in digital format that can be accessed online anywhere in the world. Google announced plans in December 2004 to digitize the libraries of the world's major university research libraries—including Oxford University, Harvard University, the University of Michigan, and the New York Public Library—to make them freely searchable online. Although it will take at least a decade to scan and catalog this library, it will include more than 15 million books that will be accessible from anywhere in the world.

The University of Texas' Harry Ransom Center has digitized a copy of the Gutenberg Bible, one of only five complete copies in the U.S. The images in this rare book, which was once accessible only to scholars, are now available to anyone anywhere in the world. (The Million Book Digital Library Project is helping preserve and provide access to the rare books of the 86 percent world in the same way.)

Digital music technologies are also creating opportunities for leapfrogging. As CD sales continue to fall, digital music (both legal and illegal) is expanding. The music industry has turned to digital-only releases of some artists, particularly those who appeal to niche audiences. This greater diversity could be especially important for the fragmented markets of the developing world. In addition, satellite radio offers many more channels and the opportunity to link audiences with common interests from around the world (as opposed to traditional, locally based broadcasts). It creates opportunities to appeal to diverse cultures and dispersed populations of developing markets.

Further developments in technology will make digital media more accessible. For example, E-ink's electronic ink, which retains its image even after power is shut off, allows the creation of e-books with sharper resolutions and lower power needs. Although the early e-book equipment based on this technology, such as Sony's Librie, is out of the range of many developing-market customers, prices should come down as the technology spreads.

With weak intellectual property protection in the developing world, digital technologies have been a cause for concern by content producers. The flip side of these intellectual property violations, however, is that they demonstrate the ability of the developing world to use digital technology to gain access to content it might not have access to through other channels. And digital products and services spread rapidly. Companies such as Samsung, with a tagline of DigitAll, have ridden this digital revolution to continued growth. How can your company use digital technologies to leapfrog into the developing world?

While health-care costs have continued to rise, telecommunications and computing costs have fallen. Telemedicine takes advantage of these trends by linking patients in rural areas or developing countries with experts in cities or other parts of the world. Gifted heart surgeon and innovator Dr. Devi Shetty in Bangalore, India, has launched a telemedicine initiative that links heart specialists in urban areas (where 75 percent of specialists are located) with clinics in rural areas. They have analyzed more than 20,000 electrocardiograms (ECGs) that were transferred electronically to experts. They have initiated thrombolytic therapy with remote patients that saved an estimated 3,000 lives in its first three years of operation. Using digital X-rays and locally developed software, they also have reduced to almost nothing the costs of chest X-rays needed to diagnose and treat tuberculosis and other diseases. "When we convert atoms into bytes, there is virtually no cost," Dr. Shetty said.

Apollo Hospitals set up a 50-bed telemedicine center in Aragnoda, a small village in south India. The center offers CT scans as well as X-ray and ECG equipment linked to specialists in other hospitals through high-speed ISDN and satellite lines. To reach the millions of people worldwide who have eye diseases, the nonprofit organization Orbis—which sponsors programs in Bangladesh, China, Ethiopia, India, and Vietnam—created the CIBER-SIGHT telemedicine project in 2002. It connects health-care professionals anywhere in the world to experts for mentoring and consultation.

Strategy #3: Create Next-Generation Technologies

The cost-benefit equation for adopting a new technology in developing countries may also be very different from that in the developed world. Solar technology, which might be less cost-effective in the heavily wired developed world, can be the low-cost solution for the developing world. Along the main road in Bangalore, Ring Road, all traffic lights are solar-powered, ultra-bright LEDs that reduce power consumption by 85 percent and remove the lights' reliance on the electric grid. By building this infrastructure from scratch, the country can leap to new technology instead of having to retrofit power-hungry incandescent traffic light systems and expensive electrical lines from central power stations.

Hewlett-Packard is testing a solar-cell fabric with photographers in South Africa. The material, which costs 80 percent less than traditional solar panels, could be used for carrying cases for cameras or other portable electronics, building the power source into the baggage. HP also has set up entrepreneurial photographers with solar-powered digital cameras and printers (as noted in Chapter 7). These photographers have been able to double their family incomes while bringing photography to remote villages that don't have electricity.

In a rural area two hours outside Durban, South Africa, a high school without electricity was wired with photovoltaic solar panels by the nonprofit Solar Electric Light Fund. The school also received computers and a satellite uplink donated by Dell and Infosat Telecommunications. After the school gained access to the Learning Channel and online resources, graduation rates shot up from 30 percent to 70 percent. Such projects demonstrate not only the technology's social power but also the market's potential. With two billion people off the energy grid, the remote rural market for solar power alone is expected to represent a $2.5 billion market globally by 2005.

New technologies could also help eliminate the need for expensive equipment such as computer screens. For example, researchers are working on high-resolution portable projectors that could be built into cell phones or PDAs, turning a blank wall into a large "flat-screen" display. This would overcome one of the major limitations of cell phones—the small display. While these innovations may be viewed as high-end gadgets in the developed world, where living rooms are already crowded with wide-screen TV sets, they represent an opportunity for leapfrogging in the developing world. This innovation could make the humble cell phone a substitute for a portable music player, camera, web browser, television, and, with a keyboard, even a computer. Already cameras are built into these phones. New technology and higher bandwidth allow users to play music, watch high-definition television or video clips, and surf the Internet.

Early-stage research on "biological" computing and power systems in developing-country labs is producing technology for extracting electricity from plants and creating opportunities for biologically based "microchips." Dr. S. P. Kosta and Y. S. Kosta at the Charolar Institute of Technology (CITC) in India proved that electricity could be extracted from plants (lighting a wristwatch lightbulb with energy extracted from leaves). They created basic electronic circuits using materials such as cactus leaves, which could form the foundation for a biological microchip. In earlier work, they also showed how the trunks of nonwoody trees such as papayas could be used as television antennas. Innovations such as these, while years or decades away from commercial products, demonstrate the potential for fundamental technological breakthroughs. These could transform life and business in developing countries, where silicon chips and power may be more scarce but vegetation is abundant. With highly trained researchers and growing research centers—and a strong motivation to innovate to meet local needs—many of these creative solutions may come from the developing world.

In automobiles, recognizing the energy and emissions problems posed by combustion engines as well as the increasingly crowded auto market in China, Chinese auto parts maker Wanxiang is working on plans for an electric automobile. In addition to addressing environmental concerns, Wanxiang founder Lu Guanqui sees a leapfrog to electric cars as a way for the company to move in front of competitors. While Japanese companies are already developing hybrids, a successful electric car at the right price still represents an opportunity for a developing-market company to be a pioneer. Developing the car will require technological breakthroughs in battery and engine technology to improve range and acceleration as well as reduce costs. The company is planning to make a substantial investment in the new technology over the coming years.

Medical innovations that are focused on the challenges of the developing world can also advance more quickly in the 86 percent markets. For example, innovations in treatments for AIDS, malaria, SARS, tuberculosis, and other diseases are coming from the developing world. Biotechnology in developing countries is benefiting from decades of investment to help these countries emerge as global players. Firms such as Biocon, Shantha Biotech, and Bharat Biotech in India have produced innovations such as the world's first recombinant human insulin for treating diabetes and a low-cost, DNA-engineered hepatitis B vaccine. With restrictions on stem cell research in the U.S., Asian countries such as Singapore, Korea, and China have emerged as global leaders of research in this area. Stem cell research is already being used in treatments in China, India, and other countries.

The higher cost of many of the drugs charged by developed countries has created the motivation for new solutions. An increasing number of innovations is coming from Indian pharmaceutical firms such as Dr. Reddy's Lab and Ranbaxy. Shouldn't the pharmaceutical companies based in the 14 percent markets think about how they can offer these markets global brands and make their drugs more affordable for patients in developing markets?

Biotech crops, now worth $44 billion per year, are grown in 18 countries, with half from developing countries. China is second only to the U.S. in supporting biotech crop research. Along with other countries in Asia, Latin America, and Africa, China is among the fastest adopters.

As these innovations indicate, developing markets can serve as a proving ground for new technology. This fact is recognized by the hundreds of companies that have set up research laboratories in China, India, and other parts of the developing world. Texas Instruments' Indian operation has received more than 200 U.S. patents. Intel's Indian subsidiary has earned more than 100, with 63 patent applications filed in 2003 alone. The number of scientific papers published by biotech researchers in Brazil and Cuba tripled between 1991 and 2002, and Chinese publications increased by seven times. More than 140,000 IT professionals work in Bangalore, surpassing Silicon Valley by about 20,000. GE's Jack F. Welch Technology Centre in Bangalore, its first and largest center outside the U.S., has already filed more than 130 patents. These leapfrogs are facilitated by a highly educated force of researchers. China, for example, graduates 250,000 engineers per year, compared to just 50,000 in the U.S. (and many of these are foreign students). Even though 39 percent of Indian adults cannot read or write, 3.2 million science students are enrolled in the country's more than 250 universities.

Strategy #4: Modify and Apply Existing Technologies in New Ways

Nuclear power, which has struggled in the West since the accidents at Three Mile Island and Chernobyl, is enjoying a revival in energy-starved China. By completely rethinking the design of the power plant, Chinese engineers have developed mini-reactors that are cleaner and safer. Because they are helium-cooled, these pebble-bed reactors can be made much smaller than the large water-cooled reactors common in the industry. The system produces hydrogen as a benign byproduct. The reactors are small enough to be purchased by a local municipality or strung together to create a more powerful energy source. Researchers expect to have the first reactor online by the end of the decade, supplementing a push to build traditional water-cooled reactors to meet the insatiable demand for energy.

By taking a different view of nuclear technology, China is helping develop a solution to its growing energy crisis. In this development, a lack of legacy systems and mind-sets is an advantage. China is not constrained by the traditional focus on water-cooled reactors. Sometimes an old technology can be rethought for a developing market. The objections that might have stalled its progress in the developed world may be less vehement. There also may be opportunities, as with the pebble-bed reactor, to rethink the technology itself.

Technologies can also be refocused on the challenges of the developing world. The ICT4B project (Information and Communications Technology for Billions), based at the University of California–Berkeley, is working on ways to string together short-range Wi-Fi systems into broader networks. With transmissions jumping from one hub or computer to another, the systems can cover miles across small villages without satellites or large central hubs. ICT4B is also developing computing devices that reduce cost and power by 10 to 100 times. Furthermore, it is creating systems that offer less-expensive intermittent connectivity to the Internet, as opposed to "always-on" systems.

An emerging technology called broadband over power lines (BPL) creates the opportunity to bring broadband access to homes through electrical wiring. This eliminates the need for coaxial cable, or even a phone line. It is still in the experimental stages in the U.S. However, further development of this technology could have significant implications for the developing world, providing broadband access to areas that have only electrical lines. The rise of Internet telephony, facilitated by satellite communications, also is making it possible to tap into the Internet to make international phone calls, all through the same broadband pipe. Net phone calls, which are seen as a way to lower phone bills in the developed world, can be a way to avoid having a phone line altogether in the developing world.

Sometimes concerns such as environmental impact can drive the switch to substitute technologies. When New Delhi switched to cleaner-burning compressed natural gas (CNG) in 2002, it replaced more than 10,000 buses. It has also converted 60,000 three-wheeled motorized rickshaws, 5,000 minibuses, and 16,000 cars to the fuel. This has created a market for these vehicles and conversion technology. Argentina now has 1.2 million CNG vehicles, Brazil has more than 600,000, and Beijing is planning to convert its buses in time for the Olympics in 2008. The shift to CNG also reduces dependence on oil, cuts operating costs, and creates opportunities for companies that supply CNG-powered vehicles. (As noted in Chapter 2, "Don't Build a Car When You Need a Bullock Cart," Hindustan Motors experienced rapid growth in urban sales of its RTV by offering a CNG version at a time when regulations were driving a switch to natural gas-powered vehicles.)

A shift to cheaper, cleaner ethanol fuel in Brazil led to a rapid increase in sales of cars that could burn both gasoline and ethanol. By 2004, Brazilians had bought more than 200,000 of these "fuel-flex" cars, accounting for about a quarter of all new car sales in the country. Companies such as Volkswagen, Fiat, General Motors, and Ford have responded to this trend to build their business in Brazil.

Strategy #5: Create Low-Cost Innovations That Mimic Other Technologies

One way to reduce costs is to create innovations that mimic other technologies but with a lower price tag. For example, the Little Smart "cell" phone system by UTStarcom in China took the country by storm by offering a low-priced cell phone based on cheaper technology. The Little Smart brand (Xiaolingtong) offers wireless local loop

(WLL) technology, which has lower quality and a narrower range than standard cell phones. This "poor man's cell phone" is actually a turbocharged cordless phone with base stations placed on city rooftops. Users cannot roam beyond their home cities, and call quality is lower, but they have access to voice mail, text messages, and other cell phone features. Usage fees are about a quarter of what subscribers pay for standard cellular service. Within three years of its launch in 1998, Little Smart had gained about 38 million users across China, accounting for two of every three new subscribers. Although it started in rural areas, it ultimately used its growing base of subscribers to enter large cities such as Beijing and Shanghai. It is exporting the system and other technologies to other developing markets in Southeast Asia, Latin America, and Africa. In 2005, it is expected to draw 40 percent of its revenues from outside China. UTStarcom's founder, Ying Wu, who came to the U.S. with just $27 to his name, has created a successful global business and a personal fortune that was worth $100 million in 2004.

Strategy #6: Develop Community Technologies

A World Bank study by economists Carsten Fink and Charles Kenny found that the digital divide may be overemphasized because many users in developing nations share cell phones or access the Internet through kiosks. When researchers measured the availability of information and communications technologies at different income levels, they found that instead of a digital divide, a "digital leapfrog" existed, because low- and middle-income countries are actually ahead of wealthy ones. While technology in the developed world tends to be individual property, companies need to realize that developing-world technology is often owned or accessed by a group. There are community televisions, shared computer terminals, and demand-pooled cell phones (as discussed in Chapter 6). Sam Pitroda, as technology advisor to former Prime Minister Rajiv Gandhi, established a network of STD telephone booths in isolated regions, which has grown to 600,000 booths. Instead of focusing on addressing the density of individual telephones, a daunting task, he realized that the key challenge was access through community phones. The project became a model for other developing countries. The implications of this are not to look just at the sale of individual products but to look at groups of users.

Households may provide technology to their domestic servants, and companies may provide laptops or Internet access to employees that they can take home. This adds to the spread of technology beyond what might seem possible based on household income.

Companies need to design strategies based on such collective approaches to technology. They also need to recognize that the opportunities for technology-related services may be far greater than the penetration of equipment or software might indicate because of multiple users and piracy. Countries may be much more connected to new technologies than they appear at first glance. Is there an opportunity to create a global chain that could be the McDonald's of Internet cafés?

Beyond Appropriate Technology

Technological advances are changing life everywhere on the planet, but probably nowhere as much as in the 86 percent markets. These technologies are moving in very quickly, without the slow process of replacing legacy systems. They also are being snatched up by consumers eager to enter the modern world. The penetration of new technologies often becomes deeper much more quickly than in the developed world. Innovations that can cut costs or tailor products to local conditions and culture are particularly critical. Many of the innovations that are needed by developing countries are being developed within these 86 percent markets. The people who have the problems are creating the solutions.

In the past, the focus of technology for developing countries sometimes has been on "appropriate" technologies that are tailored to their market limitations. These may be technologies that are less developed, designed to meet these populations on the way up. But now the focus is shifting from "appropriate" technologies to "leapfrog" technologies. Government leaders, nongovernmental organizations (NGOs), and companies are realizing that they can create low-cost solutions that are even more advanced than those of the developed world. These technologies and creative strategies are the launchpad for leapfrogging. Companies that can recognize, create, or utilize these technologies can develop businesses that leapfrog with the development of these markets.

The 86 Percent Solution

- For a specific product and market, consider how can you use new technologies to leapfrog over infrastructure challenges and build your business.

- Look at the speed of adoption of new technologies in developing markets. How will this rapid adoption facilitate selling technology products or other products and services that rely on these technologies?

- Consider opportunities to digitize your product or service to make it spread more rapidly.

- Develop innovations that mimic other technologies at a lower cost.

- Bridge the digital divide by using villages and other communities to pool resources.

- Look at ways to use the developing world as a proving ground for new technology.

9

TAKE THE MARKET TO THE PEOPLE

With many parts of developing markets virtually inaccessible by traditional distribution systems, companies have had to go out to the market with bicycles, hole-in-the-wall stores, and local knowledge to take the market to the people.

Kwame knocks on the door of a warehouse in Accra, Ghana. He is a "boreholer" taking Unilever products to a set of remote villages several hours from the capital. After speaking with a manager, Kwame fills a backpack with small packets of shampoos, soaps, toothpaste, and other items. He then heads to the bus station. As he waits, he notes with some pride that a television in the bus terminal is showing advertising for his products. This makes his work easier.

He rides the bus for two hours into the rural interior of the country. At the bus stop, he purchases a Coke from a gas station and store that has a refrigerator running on a small, noisy generator. Kwame then walks a half hour to the central village where he lives, stopping along the way to offer his wares to small villages and huts. With a working cell phone and extra batteries, he also offers the villagers individual cell phone calls as a small side business. He reaches the central village in time for an Ashanti religious festival and market day. Kwame spreads his shampoo, toothpaste, and other products on a blanket among traditional foods, cloth, and jewelry.

As the streets fill up with jostling crowds, he thinks about how far he is from the sophisticated streets of Accra. Yet, with his products spread out in front of him, he also feels so near.

Companies in developing markets are connected to customers by long and winding roads, if there are roads at all. Ghana is a country with a per capita gross national income (GNI) of about $300, and yet through boreholers and other innovations, Unilever has been able to build a multimillion-dollar business there. Ghana has a poorly developed retail network, often consisting of small stores, if there are stores at all. Without clear and easy routes to customers, companies need to find innovative methods, including boreholers such as Kwame, to take the market to the people.

Founded in 1945 in Mexico City by Lorenzo Servitje, Bimbo Bakeries has become one of the world's largest bakeries with one of the most extensive distribution networks on the American continent. To deliver its fresh bread and other products daily to 690,000 points of sale in many countries in Latin America, the U.S., and even the Czech Republic, it deploys a fleet of 26,000 vehicles. They travel a distance daily that is equivalent to circling the globe 39 times. This fleet is more than a fourth the size of the global UPS fleet (88,000).

Yet many of Bimbo's products in Mexico still go to small family stores, called *tiendas de la esquinas,* often housed in rooms within the family home. Bimbo uses sophisticated satellite tracking and handhelds to monitor inventory at individual stores. Every week a statistics report from every store ensures the right product flows into the store. There are four sets of statistics, for ordinary days, holidays, summer, and winter. (Bread consumption is higher in the winter because it is usually served with hot chocolate.)

Its distribution network has helped Bimbo, named for the bear featured in the company logo, become the largest food company in Mexico. The bakery business and related companies of Grupo Bimbo employ more than 60,000 people with annual sales of over $4 billion in 2003. Since the mid-1980s, Bimbo has continued to expand throughout Latin America and followed the emigrating Hispanic population into the U.S. Grupo Bimbo began importing products to the U.S. in the 1970s. In 1998, the company acquired Mrs. Baird's Bakeries. Today Bimbo Bakeries USA, with headquarters in Fort Worth, Texas, operates 17 plants in California, Texas, and Ohio, with more than 5,300 employees.

Retail distribution networks in Mexico continue to develop. Wal-Mart, known as Walmex in Mexico, is growing rapidly, with

2004 sales of more than US$11.8 billion in more than 690 stores in 71 cities. Led by Oxxo and 7-Eleven, Mexico had more than 6,000 convenience stores by early 2005, with annual sales of more than $2.5 billion. While the retail distribution networks in countries such as Mexico, China, and India are developing rapidly, they are still highly fragmented, particularly the farther one travels from the major centers. These fragmented distribution networks and poorly developed distribution systems require innovative solutions.

Complex Distribution

Distribution systems in the developing world are not pretty. The cities are dotted with networks of small neighborhood stores such as the *tiendas de la esquinas* of Mexico. Distribution to small villages is even more complicated. More than half of India's villages are inaccessible by motor vehicle. This means that there are no express mail trucks—no trucks at all—no trains, no cars. This makes traditional approaches to distribution in these villages much more expensive than in developed areas, often greater than the revenue from product sales. Hindustan Lever estimated that the cost per contact of promoting a product in the countryside is four to five times higher than in the cities. Even the best conventional distribution systems have been unable to penetrate beyond about one-sixth of India's rural villages.

So why bother trying to connect with these rural markets? They are where most of the population can be found. Some 70 percent of India's population lives in its more than 600,000 villages, and about 90 percent of these villages have populations of less than 2,000 (and 42 percent have populations of a mere 500 or less). Thirty-five cities in India have populations of greater than 1 million. Middle-class and wealthy households have quickly increased in smaller cities such as Vijayawada, Nagpur, and Ahmedabad. This expanding market is why KFC and Pizza Hut restaurants (Yum! Brands), Reebok International, Bacardi, Ford, Nokia, and other companies are pushing deeper into India's second-tier cities. In China, two-thirds of the population, some 800 million people, live in rural areas, and companies are increasingly looking to small cities and villages for opportunities. (In Latin America, however, urban development has brought 75 percent of populations to the cities, creating its own infrastructure problems.) Companies that focus only on large cities such as Mumbai or Beijing are ignoring most of the people in the market.

While traditional mechanisms for distribution may be either unavailable or too expensive, companies such as Bimbo and Unilever are finding rich opportunities by using innovative approaches to solve "last-mile" challenges. Developing markets have their own distribution networks, but they might look nothing like the sophisticated distribution systems of developed markets. Rural villagers have social networks that can facilitate market-building. Although the channels may not be as efficient as selling through a major retail chain, with the right strategies, these channels can create a way to reach the many diffused consumers in developing markets.

Strategies for Taking the Market to the People

How can companies take the market to the people? Managers need to rethink and redesign their value chains to meet the distinctive demands of developing markets. While every market has particular features that need to be addressed, common characteristics across the 86 percent markets shape go-to-market strategies.

Strategy #1: Position for the Paanwalla

Small shops called paanwallas are crammed into virtually every nook and cranny of Indian cities, similar to the sari-sari stores in the Philippines or the *tiendas de la esquinas* of Mexico. "Paan" means "after lunch or dinner." These small stores started out by selling beetlenuts, cigarettes, and other products that might be purchased on a walk after dinner. These shops now account for about one-third of the 6 million retail outlets in the nation. And while local and global chain stores and malls are growing rapidly, they contributed just 3 percent of India's total retail revenues in 2004. The sari-sari stores in the Philippines account for nearly 90 percent of the nation's retail outlets and grew more than 11 percent in 2003. There were more than half a million of these stores, compared to less than 1,000 supermarkets. These small stores in different parts of the world have long hours and a presence in almost every corner of the country. Shop owners have strong relationships with their local community, and they even offer informal credit to customers. This creates intense loyalty from customers who frequent the shops at least once a day.

The importance of paanwallas in local commerce has led to the addition of other frequently replenished products such as bread and soft drinks, cell phones, batteries, detergents, and shampoos. As companies have recognized the importance of these outlets, fierce competition has resulted for the limited shelf space in the 8-by-10-foot stores (see Figure 9-1). Although Pepsi markets through just 50,000 of the roughly 2 million paanwalla shops in India, this channel accounts for more than 10 percent of the company's total sales. This is an ideal place for taking everyday products such as cigarettes and soda to India's growing lower-middle-class segment.

FIGURE 9-1 While large retailers such as Wal-Mart are growing rapidly, distribution in developing countries is often through tiny shops such as this one in Ghana.

Similarly, in China, most distribution is handled through tiny stores. In Ningbo, for example, on China's eastern coast, a network of 6,000 tiny independent street-corner shops account for 90 percent of beer distribution. The local KK brand, with a distribution system designed to quickly deliver cases of beer to these independent distribution points, controls 90 percent of the market. The local brands fly off the shelves of these small shops while a few neglected bottles from global power brands sit past their expiration dates.

Strategy #2: Create Multiple Levels of Distribution

Companies often set up multiple levels of distribution to reach different parts of the market. For example, Hindustan Lever in India set up several programs to progressively extend its reach from urban centers. It first established a program called "Indirect Coverage" in the late

1960s, targeting retailers in accessible villages close to urban markets. Since Hindustan Lever was the only one targeting these markets, village retailers had to travel to urban areas if they wanted to purchase competitors' products, giving Hindustan Lever a substantial advantage.

In the 1990s, the company launched its next wave of rural distribution through an initiative dubbed "Streamline." The company appointed rural distributors who, in turn, appointed "Star Sellers" in neighboring villages. A Star Seller would use local transport vehicles such as motorcycles, rickshaws, Jeeps, or even bullock carts to take products to retailers in smaller villages. Streamline thus expanded the company's reach in India to markets that were previously considered inaccessible.

Still, much of rural India remained out of reach of this distribution system, with almost 500,000 Indian villages still untapped. Hindustan Lever then launched a new program to penetrate more deeply into these rural markets. "Project Shakti," rolled out in 2000, is based on a direct-to-home model organized around self-help groups—groups of 10 to 15 underprivileged rural women set up by the government or nongovernmental organizations (NGOs). Through Project Shakti, a Sanskrit word that means "power," these women become brand ambassadors in "media-dark" rural villages, communicating the benefits of brand and category use. This personal communication and distribution channel is particularly effective in an environment that is largely untouched by electronic media and has high rates of illiteracy.

India has more than 1 million self-help groups, and their numbers are growing rapidly. These groups have access to microcredit, but with little opportunity for microenterprise, because few business opportunities exist. Project Shakti promoted local development while allowing Hindustan Lever to penetrate into smaller villages in India. By 2005, the company's goal is to have more than 25,000 trained "Shakti Entrepreneurs" covering over 100,000 villages and touching the lives of 100 million rural consumers. This would double the company's reach in rural India.

Efficient rural distribution systems have also been created by public agencies such as India's Anganwadi system for distributing medicines, condoms, and other health information and supplies. For every 25 villages, there is one central health-care center, which has vans for carrying supplies to villages as well as skilled staff. Village Auxiliary Nurse Midwives carry out the campaign and disseminate the products. The government also has established a Public Distribution Service (PDS) network to provide commodities such as kerosene, cooking oil, sugar, and grains to rural households. The outlets are open two or three hours per day, and employees are paid in food.

Strategy #3: Use Distribution Bubbles to Find Customers When *They Are There*

In contrast to permanent retail outlets in developed markets, developing-market distribution, particularly in rural areas, is often through temporary channels such as carnivals and market days, or vans that roll into a village and create a market. These are like bubbles that appear on the surface of a lake for a moment and then disappear. Companies need to be astute in finding and capitalizing on them to be where the market is when it is there. For example, every year, indigenous Berbers of North Africa stream out of the mountains for an annual three-day festival near Imilchil in Morocco. The festival draws Berbers from throughout the region for three days of frenetic trading as the self-sufficient mountain people stock up on staples. For this market, there may be one shot every year.

In Ghana, Unilever built multiple levels of distribution as it did in India (as discussed earlier). But after creating a network of key distributors and subdistributors that allowed it to reach 80 percent of the country's rural retail outlets, Unilever turned its attention to less-permanent and less-formal channels. In 2003, Unilever added rural sales reps (boreholers) to distribute products to remote villages with rotational markets (market days) that are difficult to put into coverage plans. These boreholers also engaged in direct selling and sampling to customers. In Ghana, where consumer purchasing power was diminishing, Unilever's business continued to grow in volume and profit.

In Indian villages, companies set up tables in the markets, playing Bollywood film music to attract crowds and offering education about the products. They also use less-frequent carnivals, such as the *melas* in India, to sell products and raise awareness (see Figure 9-2). While the developed world may concentrate on distribution through stores, the developing world has a much more complex and fluid structure. Companies need to adapt to this structure to find the markets where and when they appear. These festivals are usually held around major religious holy days, which often vary from region to region within a given country.

FIGURE 9-2 Carnivals such as the "melas" in India offer opportunities for marketing and distribution for companies that know how to use them.

Companies can also create such market opportunities in conjunction with local governments. For example, international fairs invite companies from different countries to set up stalls to showcase their products in India. Why couldn't these fairs, now held in the cities, be extended to more rural areas as well, taking globalization to the heartland?

Strategy #4: Take the Bank Out of the Branch

Foreign banks in India are restricted by law to a limited number of branches in a few cities. So Citibank created Citibank Suvidha, a bank without branches (suvidha means "facility"). Since customers can't come to a branch, the bank goes to customers' homes. Citibank uses vans and a network of 9,000 direct-selling agents in five cities, called Citi Friends, to promote its credit cards, loans, and other services through visits to customers' homes. While home visits reduce the need for branches and other physical infrastructure for the banks, customers see this personal attention as a status symbol. The bank also has a network of automatic teller machines in Bangalore, but these ATMs are more like virtual branches, with security guards and hostesses who help new users operate the stand-alone ATMs. The low overhead of the branchless bank has allowed minimum deposits to be reduced from 10,000 rupees (US$224) for a typical bank to just 1,000 rupees (US$22). From one "branch" in Bangalore, the bank has grown to serve 600,000 clients in the city and a total of 1 million clients across India. Drawing on Citibank's skill in retail lending, the bank has also become a major force in providing small loans. In rural villages in India, microlender BASIX has set up simplified ATMs with a local host to help villagers use this local "branch."

India's Kotak Bank has taken this one step further, offering free home delivery and pickup of cash (in amounts as small as 5,000 rupees, or about US$115) to its standard savings customers. This is a service most banks offer to only their high-net-worth clients, but it makes sense in a country with a low penetration of banks and credit cards. Space is tight, branches are hard to establish, labor is relatively cheap, and population density is high. This changes the business model for banking, which has been focused on establishing good retail locations. A delivery service means that location is less important. (How many U.S. customers know where their local Domino's outlet is located?) Why offer only pizza for home delivery? Why not banking services? What other products and services could be brought to customers' doors?

Strategy #5: Develop On-the-Ground Insights

While distribution in every developing market is complicated, each market is complex in its own way. By understanding and adapting to local regulations and conditions, Aramex International grew from two small offices in Amman, Jordan and New York in 1982 to a nearly $200 million global full-service transportation and logistics company with 3,400 employees in 125 offices in 37 countries in 2004. "The Middle East is 22 countries, and each country has its own laws, own way of doing things, and own strategy toward the private sector," said Aramex CEO Fadi Ghandour. In Tunisia, for example, all deliveries have to be made through the postal service, so the only way to do business there is to contract with the post office. Some countries have special courier taxes, and others have restrictions on foreign ownership.

Local knowledge and staff are crucial to understanding these complex local regulations and systems. Aramex sets up operations based on a federated model with local CEOs. "The people who work for us are from the region," Ghandour said. "Some of these obstacles may worry Western investors, but the people there grew up in the region, and they understand how to do business there, regardless of the political risk. They do not find the civil war in Lebanon or Iraq invading Kuwait as a risk from a physical perspective. These are the sons and daughters of these countries. These are their homes." Aramex was among the first companies to enter Iraq after the U.S.-led invasion in 2003, just 10 days after the invasion ended.

"We trained people in Jordan before the war, and the minute it ended and we were able to establish trucking service, we could operate immediately," Ghandour said. "There already is some business in Iraq, and we are committed to the market. There are 5 million people in Baghdad, and they are not sitting at home doing nothing."

Aramex found that there was an advantage to the complexity and instability of many of these markets because it created an initial entry barrier for rivals. The importance of such on-the-ground insights can be seen in DHL's decision in November 2004 to purchase a majority stake in Blue Dart, India's top domestic courier service.

Companies have to adapt distribution to the demands of local regulations as well. A 1998 ban on door-to-door selling in China cut off Avon from its traditional personal selling. So it began selling products through small "beauty boutiques" and at counters in hypermarkets and department stores. (As part of complying with World Trade Organization guidelines, the Chinese government was expected to lift the ban in 2005.)

Strategy #6: Create Distribution Systems from Scratch

British-born engineer Nancy Abeiderrahmane created a new distribution system, based on grassroots networks, to build a supply chain for Africa's first camel's milk dairy in the West-African nation of Mauritania. Before the dairy was created in 1989, camel's milk was sold at the roadside from buckets. In the hot climate, milk spoiled rapidly. Although the milk was a staple of nomadic herdsmen, health concerns and the rising urban population led to an increasing dependence on imported ultra-pasteurized, long-life cow's milk. The nation was importing more than 50,000 tons of sterilized and powdered milk from Europe each year. Camel's milk offered benefits over cow's milk, including increased potassium, iron, magnesium, and vitamin C, and low cholesterol. It is less allergenic and good for diabetes. What was lacking was an effective system for collection, pasteurization, and distribution.

Abeiderrahmane's Tiviski Dairy and its delivery system have made camel's milk a healthy drink for city dwellers while providing valuable income to nomadic herdsmen. The system begins with a network of suppliers who collect camel's milk from camps and villages each morning and deliver it to a plant outside the Mauritanian capital of Nouakchott. The milk is pasteurized, packaged, chilled, and shipped the same morning, using a fleet of vans that deliver the product to the countless corner shops in the region. Cartons of milk are regularly air-freighted to the city of Nouadhibou in the north, are taken by road to the town of Rosso in the south, and are even shipped by boat to neighboring Senegal. Success, however, ultimately depends on the city's small corner grocery stores having electricity to keep the pasteurized milk cool.

Tiviski's sales more than tripled between 1993 and 2002, when production reached 20,000 liters per day (before a severe drought hit the sector). The dairy's expanded product line, particularly cheese, offered a platform for further growth. A German importer offered to buy the entire camel cheese production from the company, but the export production of this "camelbert" cheese was blocked by European Union (EU) regulations. These regulations, designed for more traditional cow and goat products, do not specifically cover camel's milk. If it hadn't been stopped by these regulatory hurdles, the successful business in this small African nation could have provided a platform for moving into the developed markets of Europe.

The debate over importing camel's milk cheese into Europe highlights some of the differences in how developed and developing nations look at the world. Although the Tiviski Dairy uses European standards of production in its dairy, tests for pasteurization of cow's milk don't work for camel's milk. EU regulators thus insisted that to ensure standards of hygiene, camels would need to be milked by machine. The Mauritanians saw this as a ludicrous proposition, given that the milk is drawn from small villages and nomadic herdsman.

Even if the technical hurdles of mechanical milking could be overcome, camels can be temperamental, known to cut off their milk production if they object to the process.

Strategy #7: Use Existing Networks Creatively

Great potential exists for using existing networks in creative ways. For example, low-cost Indian airline Air Deccan developed a system for selling airline tickets through gas stations, bank ATMs, and mobile phones. This has allowed the airline to tap into a network of 6,000 HPCL gasoline stations, many of which already had Internet connections that facilitated the sales, and also a growing network of ATMs and cell phones. This has made it easier for customers, many of whom have never flown before, to purchase tickets using cash or credit.

Other companies have found creative ways to reach their markets. Banco Azteca in Mexico, targeting the 16 million households that have a monthly income between $250 and $1,300, set up branches in Grupo Elektra appliance stores. The largest appliance retailer in the country, Grupo Elektra sells about 70 percent of its merchandise on credit, so it made sense to establish bank branches in its stores. The bank also has invested in high-tech fingerprint readers to ensure security for customers who don't carry ID cards or passbooks. Furthermore, it employs a team of 3,000 loan officers on motorcycles. Although loan recipients might pay only $8 per week, the bank earns 48 percent interest and boasts a 97 percent repayment rate.

Elle 18, a youth brand of nail enamel, lipsticks, and other cosmetics in India, sells its products through Barista coffee shops, a favorite hangout of high school and college students. This is not an expected distribution point for cosmetics, but it represents a creative way to repurpose the existing distribution infrastructure.

South African beer distribution initially depended on backyard pubs called "shebeens" that offered their own moonshine brews served in old jam tins. Until 1962, black South Africans were prohibited from purchasing commercially brewed beer. When the prohibition was lifted, South African Breweries (SAB) used the local shebeens and other small outlets to build its business, providing almost all the beer sold through these outlets. SAB developed a network of drivers who could deliver products along rough rural roads, often setting up its former employees in their own trucking businesses. Leaving nothing to chance, the company also needed to make sure its rural distributors had refrigerators and even generators to keep the refrigerators running.

The company used such strategies to build its business one shebeen at a time through South Africa and other countries in the region. SAB ultimately acquired Miller Brewing Company in the U.S. in 2002, becoming the second-largest brewing company in the world (by volume). The company's creative strategies allowed it to move from a small developing market to a business spanning 40 countries, including a significant presence in China, India, many African nations, and other developing countries.

Companies need a wide range of methods to reach different parts of the market. Coca-Cola's distribution fleet in India ranges from 10-ton trucks to open-bay three-wheelers that can navigate the narrow alleyways of Indian cities to trademarked tricycles and pushcarts. Coca-Cola also uses backpack dispensers at crowded cricket games. A project by the Indian Institute of Technology in Kapur has created a bicycle rickshaw bearing a computer with high-speed Internet access that can be pedaled into small villages, accompanied by a computer instructor to teach computing to local villagers. Another pilot project uses a pedal-powered cab to help doctors in the city provide videoconference consults to distant villages. Although these are social development projects, they illustrate the creative approaches that are sometimes needed to reach developing markets.

One of the most remarkable examples of the creative use of existing networks is the phenomenal "dabbawala system" of delivering lunches across Mumbai, India. It is probably the world's most efficient lunch delivery system. A cooperative run by illiterate and semiliterate entrepreneurs, it uses railroads, cars, bicycles, and carriers on foot to collect 175,000 home-cooked meals from workers' homes and deliver them to their offices. (It is a tradition for Indian workers to have home-cooked meals delivered to work.) The lunches in tiffin boxes, or "dab," are collected from homes between 7 and 9 a.m. and are delivered by train, bicycle, and foot to offices by 12:30 p.m.

This 120-year-old system uses an elegant "packet switching" system. Each metal carrier, called a tiffin box, has a code marked on it that directs it through a network of teams of deliverers, known as dabbawalas. The box often exchanges hands three or four times on the way to its destination. The system is nearly error-free, with an estimated one mistake for every eight million deliveries. And this remarkable journey costs just 150 to 300 rupees (about $3.50 to $7) per month, depending on location and collection time. This demonstrates the possibilities for developing very creative and flexible distribution systems using the existing infrastructure of rail, road, and sidewalk.

Seeing Opportunities That Are Off the Grid

Since much of the population of the developing world is "off the grid," the challenge is to connect companies to the market. Most of the opportunities in developing markets are in small cities or rural villages. To reach these diffused markets, companies have to rethink their approaches to distribution. Costs need to be streamlined, but this can often be done by applying information technology, wireless communications, and networks of small entrepreneurial distributors. Every dollar invested needs to be justified in value created for extremely cost-conscious end consumers.

Major retailers are expanding rapidly in the developing world, changing the competitive landscape. Wal-Mart had established 40 stores in Chinese cities by 2004 and planned 15 more in 2005, as many other global and domestic retailers moved in or expanded their positions in the market. In the long run, Wal-Mart, Tesco, Carrefour, and other global firms, as well as local chains, will continue to consolidate distribution channels, as they have done in developed markets. But in the near term, products will flow through many fragmented retail outlets and directly into rural villages. It is vital to understand these channels and how they can be used to connect to the market.

Companies need to recognize and take advantage of the idiosyncratic distribution systems that already exist in these markets. These systems may look nothing like those of developed countries. Companies may need to distribute through the small paanwalla stores, use innovative approaches such as the dabbawala lunch distribution system, or create systems from scratch.

The 86 Percent Solution

- Design distribution systems to reach the paanwallas, *tiendas de la esquinas*, and other small outlets of the developing world. How do you need to rethink your supply chain and products?

- Look for local partners or entrepreneurial networks who can understand and connect with local markets.

- Explore opportunities to create multiple levels of distribution to serve the cities and rural areas.

- Find temporary distribution points such as market days and festivals, and design strategies for these distribution "bubbles."

- Examine the impact of local regulations and restrictions. How do you need to rethink your distribution systems in light of these obstacles?

- Look at buses, trains, and other existing transportation systems to identify creative "dabbawala" opportunities to move your products to market.

10 ――――――――――――――

DEVELOP WITH
THE MARKET

**Developing markets are a moving target, so companies
need to evolve their strategies with the market.**

*Soo never imagined her children would be watching televi-
sion on her LG refrigerator in Seoul, South Korea. Because
a video camera is installed in the same refrigerator door,
she can also log on to the Internet and look in on her
younger child while she is at work. Gone are the days when
children's drawings—except for the digital variety—
covered the shiny metal door. Her teenage son plays multi-
player games on the flat-screen computer in the living
room, where he also uses high-speed Internet access to*

*download music, videos, and books from just about any-
where in the world. When Soo was born in 1963, the country's per capita GNP was just $100; today it is pushing
$10,000, making South Korea the 12th largest economy in
the world.*

*The irony is that Soo's sister, Min, who moved to the U.S. a
decade ago in search of opportunities, still has only dialup
Internet access. Min doesn't have a computer in her refrigerator; she was glad to buy a model with a built-in ice-
maker. By 2004, some 75 percent of South Korean
households had broadband access, while only 20 percent of
homes in the U.S. did. Soo also can watch television on her
GSM cell phone when she's stuck in traffic or waiting in
line at the store. Of course, she waits in fewer lines today
because she pays all her bills through her cell phone. She
hasn't been in a bank in ages. The world is moving so
rapidly. Soo smiles to think that she was jealous when Min
left for a U.S. university and a new life nearly a decade ago.
Soo's home may be a little smaller, but her technology and
quality of life have rapidly caught and surpassed that of
her American sister. Now Min is jealous—and is actually
thinking about bringing her family back home.*

*With 48 million people, South Korea is much smaller than
the billion-plus populations of countries such as China and
India. Even so, it took South Korea about four decades to
climb into the $10,000 club. Along the way, consumers and
society underwent fundamental changes. Through this
process of development, powerful new businesses and
brands emerged, such as Samsung and LG. Companies
that can understand these changes and adapt to them have
an opportunity to develop with the market.*

Emerging markets do not stand still. Incomes and gross domestic product (GDP) continue to rise. By definition, a "developing" nation continues to develop. It may take decades, but during that time, the market keeps changing and offering fresh opportunities. The strategies that work today may not be successful tomorrow. As markets continue to develop, they undergo a set of changes, often somewhat predictable, that shape their future direction. Understanding and anticipating these patterns of change—and the other opportunities presented by development—can help companies create effective solutions and profitable businesses.

Strategies for Developing with the Market

How can companies recognize shifts and transformations in developing markets and take advantage of them? How can they export their successes from one culture to another? They can use a number of strategies to keep up with change.

Strategy #1: Look for Patterns of Change

As markets move from $1,000 per capita GNP to $5,000 to $10,000, they go through certain natural stages. These changes create new opportunities. Although every nation follows its own trajectory of development, economic evolution has predictable phases. Each of these shifts creates new opportunities or could signal a point at which a company needs to change its positioning or direction. Some shifts are predictable, such as the empowerment of women and the emergence of a consumer culture as economies mature. With rising incomes, consumers rise through Abraham Maslow's "hierarchy of needs" as they shift from focusing on basic survival to concern for safety, love, esteem, and self-actualization.[1] Other similarities in development are based on geography and religious and cultural traditions. By recognizing these patterns, companies can anticipate shifts as they build or transform their businesses.

To visualize these changes, think about the differences in countries at different points in this trajectory. For example, compare the above-US$30,000 per capita GNP of the U.S. and many European nations to that of a newly developed country such as South Korea that has just joined the US$10,000 club. Then compare a country with a mid-range per capita GNP, such as Mexico (about US$6,000), to a country just pushing US$1,000, such as China, and sub-US$1,000 economies such as India and Ghana. Development economists have offered more complex theories about what happens to countries as they develop, but this simple exercise can provide insights into the changes and the opportunities they present.

Look at the histories of current developed nations, and identify some of the key transition points. Then look for signs of these shifts in the country of interest. If such a shift took place, how would your strategy need to change? A few examples of shifts on the way to development are the rise in prepared foods as women enter the workforce, the rise of environmental concern with industrial expansion, and pressures on infrastructure. China already has experienced shifts in attitudes toward sex, marriage, and divorce that have led to fundamental social changes, including a divorce rate that has risen from 3 percent in the 1970s to 14 percent today. Global television shows such as the popular *telenovelas* in Brazil have changed social mores, broaching touchy issues such as interracial marriage and women's empowerment.

As economies develop, consumers increasingly take charge. They demand better products and service quality. With rising competition for their disposable income, they will become increasingly choosy as a consumer culture develops. Companies need to pay attention to these changes and modify their approaches to business accordingly.

Economic development is just one of the drivers of change. Significant social shifts occur as well, some of which are related to economic progress. In Iran, for example, where dogs have long been considered "impure," acceptance of dogs as pets is increasing, and ownership is rising. Owners had traditionally been subject to fines or harassed when walking their dogs in public (although the religious taboo against dogs in the writings of spiritual leader Ayatollah Ruhollah Khomeini was never formally written into law). The use of dogs in drug interventions and search-and-rescue operations has helped soften public perceptions. These more favorable views of pets can be seen in the first government-sanctioned pet show held in Tehran in September 2004. Such trends are important to monitor. Imagine the opportunities for pet foods and other products that would be created by widespread pet ownership. (The U.S. market alone spends more than $32 billion annually on pets, and the U.S. population of pets surpassed the population of people in 2003.)

Strategy #2: Develop Solutions with Government, NGOs, and Other Players

As emerging markets develop, governments, foundations, and non-governmental organizations (NGOs) play a central role in the development. The Narayana Hrudayalaya medical foundation, building on a network of hospitals, has spearheaded a rural health insurance initiative for India's poor at a phenomenal 11 cents per month. Through this health-care plan, it is already offering free medical treatment to more than 2 million farmers in the Indian state of Karnataka.

Public-private partnerships are critical in addressing other social and economic challenges. To address iodine deficiencies, in 2000 Unilever worked with UNICEF and the Ghana Health Service to introduce the low-cost iodized salt Annapurna (drawing on its success with an earlier campaign in India). The company made the salt available in 100-gram sachets for the equivalent of about 6 cents

(500 Ghanaian cedis), low enough to be purchased by the poorest customers. This initiative helped double the use of iodized salt in Ghana between 1998 and 2002, from 28 percent to 50 percent, an additional 4 million people.

By working together, the partners created a win-win situation. UNICEF and the Ghana Health Service made significant progress toward their goals of reducing iodine deficiency, while Unilever turned a profit within 18 months, two years ahead of schedule. It gained half the market for salt in the country. The company is now planning to introduce the product in other African countries, as well as other products such as biscuits fortified with vitamin A and zinc. Unilever also is working with NGOs in Ghana to create an entire local market and distribution ecosystem for oil produced from the nuts of the abundant Allanblackia tree as a substitute for more expensive palm oil in products such as soaps and margarine. This would help the local economy while offering a cheaper source of oil.

Rigorous business methods are also being applied to policy issues. Ashoka, a global foundation developed by Bill Drayton, a former McKinsey & Co. consultant, is promoting "social entrepreneurship" projects around the globe. It supports the work of 1,500 Ashoka Fellows in 53 countries, who have affected the lives of millions of people. The Naandi Foundation (*naandi* means "new beginning") is using a strategy of "public-private convergence" to engage governments, corporations, academic institutions, communities, and other stakeholders in India. The foundation—created by prominent business leaders in Hyderabad working with the government of Andhra Pradesh—has successfully implemented several initiatives. These include improving water supplies, schools, food, security, employment, and health care for more than 300,000 people in India. Katha, a nonprofit foundation promoting literacy in India, joined with Tata Group, British Telecom, Intel, and other corporate and government leaders to launch an initiative to bring IT technologies to rural schools and communities.

Major foundations from the developed world are using professionalism to address economic and social issues. For example, the Bill & Melinda Gates Foundation commissioned a study in India that found that one of the major sources of the spread of AIDS was through sex workers and lonely long-distance truck drivers. It then worked with governments and other organizations to establish a chain of 50 clinics at truck stops to promote safe sex among the three million commercial sex workers and five million truck drivers in high-risk areas. This is a major part of the foundation's $200 million, five-year Avahan AIDS prevention initiative. Led by McKinsey & Company veteran Ashok Alexander, this initiative is helping shape public policy in the country that has the second-highest number of people infected with the disease. Gates and other sophisticated foundations use rigorous strategies to achieve the most impact with their investments and use auditing to ensure that money spent for vaccines and other treatments is not wasted or stolen. The Michael & Susan Dell Foundation has an endowment of more than $1 billion for children's health, education, safety, and development initiatives. In November 2004, it gave a $1 million grant to WaterPartners International, an innovative nonprofit that expects to provide clean water to more than 200,000 children and adults in India over the next decade. The Gates Foundation and governments around the world also have committed $1.5 billion to childhood vaccinations in the world's poorest nations.

Communities of the very poor in developing countries are organizing themselves to address their own needs. Rising populations of urban poor living in slums, facing eviction from homes or demolition of temporary structures, have begun to organize to improve their living conditions. For example, in Mumbai, India, the Society for the Promotion of Area Resource Centers (SPARC), founded by Sheela Patel, and the National Slum Dwellers Federation worked with slum dwellers to secure land, housing, and infrastructure for the urban poor.

As discussed in Chapter 3, "Aim for the Ricochet Economy," immigrants abroad also make substantial contributions to the development of their home countries through donations and investments. Companies and nonprofit organizations can work together to facilitate these flows. For example, after the devastating tsunami and earthquake in December 2004 that killed more than 100,000 people in Southeast Asia, Indian community website Sulekha.com decided to help. It raised more than $500,000 in three days for relief efforts from members of its online community around the world in partnership with the Association for India's Development (AID).

Strategy #3: Export Successes

Solutions for one developing market can often be exported to other developing markets that have similar income constraints and environments. For example, Indian carmaker Maruti Udyog's Alto model (created with partner Suzuki) has been a hit in Europe, and its lower-priced models have moved successfully from its home market to other developing markets. The economy model Maruti 800 has been a success in countries such as Chile, Uruguay, Algeria, Egypt, Sri Lanka, Yugoslavia, and Malta. The versatile Omni was taken to Kenya, Mozambique, Cyprus, and Nepal. The four-wheel-drive Gypsy is a front-runner in the segment in many African and Asian markets. Chinese automaker Chery also is reaching out. It launched a factory in Iran in 2004, and it is looking at operations in Poland, Malaysia, Pakistan, Egypt, Venezuela, and Syria. The vehicles designed for its domestic markets appeal to the broader developing world.

The opportunities and challenges of creating a "world car" were demonstrated by Fiat's Palio, built for the Brazilian market in 1996. It had European engineering adapted to the demands of Brazilian roads and tastes. It was an initial success. Between 1981 and 1999, while the Brazilian auto market grew by 225 percent, Fiat grew even faster, posting 487 percent growth. By 2000, Fiat had sold more than 1.5 million

Palio models to customers in 41 markets, including Germany, Italy, France, Spain, South Africa, Morocco, Russia, Vietnam, and India. Fiat demonstrated that by creating a successful product for one developing market, it could expand into others. But the Palio's progress ultimately slowed with financial crises in Asia, Eastern Europe, and Latin America, as well as with rising competition. This revealed the precarious nature of success, particularly in developing markets.

Every segment has opportunities to transfer successes from one developing country to another. Romanian company Dacia, acquired by Renault, launched its Logan model in 2004. It is designed for the rough roads, harsh climates, heavy use, and tight purses of middle-class families in developing markets. With a price tag of 5,700 euros (about US$7,500), the car features high ground clearance, a large trunk, dust filters, and easy maintenance. In addition to Romanian sales, Renault planned to export this "world car" to Colombia, Russia, Morocco, Iran, and, later, China and India. Even two-wheelers can make the leap to new markets. Indian scooter maker Bajaj, after creating a low-priced but well-built scooter for its domestic market, expanded its exports to the Middle East, Asia, and even the U.S. These sales helped it grow at 50 percent per year, with a target of 500,000 vehicles exported annually by 2007.

Specialized products and segments also can find opportunities across markets. Armored cars from Brazil, tested under tough conditions, have become a huge export, making Brazil the world's top producer of bulletproof vehicles by 2001, with orders going to developing countries such as Iraq. Bahrat Electronics and Electronics Corp. in India, which developed a $200 battery-operated voting machine for the 2004 elections, creating a $200 million domestic business, were exploring applications in countries such as Sri Lanka, Mauritius, and Singapore.

Finally, as noted in Chapter 4, "Connect Brands to the Market," global brands and celebrities can transfer across markets. Bollywood actress and former Miss World Aishwarya Rai has become a global celebrity through her 24 films, first in the developing world and then in the developed world. She has been compared to film legends such as Grace Kelly and Ingrid Bergman. The social networks discussed in Chapter 3 can also help transfer products and services around the world. For example, ICICI Bank in India launched a successful promotion on Sulekha.com. It offered visitors $2 discounts on Bollywood movie tickets in exchange for allowing the bank to contact them about setting up an account for relatives in India. These and other campaigns helped ICICI bank gain 20 percent market share in the U.S. among nonresident Indians.

Strategy #4: Look for Opportunities for "Reverse Colonialization"

Surprisingly, the remnants of earlier colonial periods can sometimes help in this process of global exporting. For example, the Portuguese culture on China's Macao peninsula has served as a gateway for Chinese business to the 220 million Portuguese-speaking people in Latin America and other parts of the world. It has helped China become Brazil's second-largest trading partner (after the U.S.) and fastest-growing export market, with trade between the two countries that ballooned to $6.7 billion in 2004. Outside of Latin America, knowledge of the Portuguese language has also strengthened China's relationships with the West African nation of Angola and with Portugal itself.

Similarly, the high concentration of English speakers in India, partly a byproduct of its past as a British colony, has helped make the country a center of back-office service and call centers for the U.S. French and English speakers in African nations are also helping drive the growth of their fledgling outsourcing business, with call centers targeting countries such as France and Britain. French-language films from Africa are also gaining a growing following in Europe and other parts of the world. Indonesian food is popular in the Netherlands, Indian food in the UK, and Moroccan food in France as a result of their colonial ties.

While the remnants of past colonialism are often a liability for countries, they sometimes can be leveraged to forge new global relationships as developing countries move into other parts of the world.

Strategy #5: Address the "Growing Pains"

Development brings with it many challenges and growing pains. The path to development is often lined with political and economic turbulence, strains on fragile infrastructure (as discussed in Chapter 7, "Bring Your Own Infrastructure"), and environmental challenges. In Beijing, planners are scurrying to build new roads to keep up with an explosion of automobiles, surpassing 2 million by the end of 2004 in this city alone. Indian drivers bought almost 1 million cars in 2003–2004. Airports and seaports in developing countries have had to be built rapidly, and roads and railroads need to be rebuilt. China's rapid expansion of air travel, topping more than 100 million air travelers by 2004, led to US$8 billion in orders for Airbus and Boeing jetliners by early 2005.

Air and water quality in China are suffering from its rapid development. Forests, climates, biological diversity, and human health are all impacted by the byproducts of development. A World Bank report found that China is suffering some of the worst soil erosion in the world. Water quality and air quality are poor and growing worse. Ninety percent of rivers flowing through Chinese cities are seriously polluted with sewage, garbage, and industrial waste. If its economy keeps growing at its current rate, China will overtake the U.S. as the world's largest source of greenhouse gases within three decades. Generators and construction create noise pollution as well.

Yet these growing pains create economic opportunities, as they have done in the developed world. Insurance and other instruments can help mitigate financial risks. Companies can help supply the needed infrastructure or offer alternatives such as low-polluting energy and equipment. China's dependence on coal fuel contributes to its air quality problems and small generators add to noise pollution, but these problems also create pressure for a shift to natural gas or solar power.

Strategy #6: Export Products to the Developed World

Developed-market segments that need rugged, low-maintenance, or low-cost products might also turn to the solutions of the developing world. Tractor maker Mahindra & Mahindra, after stress-testing its designs and products in the rural Indian market, moved into the U.S. market, targeting part-time farmers who use the tractors for hobbies or small farms. The small and efficient tractors created for the smaller farms of developing markets were a good fit for these American farmers.

New global powerhouses are moving from the developing world to the developed world. Among them are Ranbaxy Laboratories in India, which has become one of the fastest-growing firms in the generic drug industry. China's TLC became the world's largest television maker when it bought RCA; it controls 19 percent of this domestic market. India's Tata Group, under the chairmanship of Ratan Tata, purchased Tyco's telecom unit. Mexico's Cemex has become one of the world's leading cement companies. Lenovo (formerly Legend) has become one of the world's leading computer makers after acquiring IBM's PC unit. These are just a few examples.

Sometimes innovative products that are designed to solve the challenges of the developing world can become hits in developed markets for different reasons. A silk-like fabric made of soybeans was created as a low-cost fabric for Chinese markets, but it spread to the developed world because it was considered environmentally friendly. After success in domestic markets, Shanghai Winshow Soybeanfiber Industry Co., founded by entrepreneur Li Guanqi, took this "soybean silk" to South Korea, the U.S., and Europe. There it is commanding a premium from consumers seeking eco-friendly fabrics.

The arts are also gaining global audiences, driven in part by the expanding expatriate populations in developed countries. This has increased the prominence and price tags of Indian artwork, for example. An auction of Indian art in December 2004 netted $2.9 million, and individual contemporary works are selling for more than $400,000.

Strategy #7: Import Customers from the Developed World

In addition to exporting products *to* the developed world, digital technologies and inexpensive travel allow developing countries to import customers *from* the developed world. Developing nations are becoming hot destinations for "medical tourists," not only from other developing nations but also from the developed world. Thailand, Malaysia, Jordan, Singapore, and India collectively host more than 1 million medical travelers each year, earning more than $1 billion in treatment costs alone. The market in India alone is expected to reach $2 billion by 2015. The economics are compelling. For example, a North Carolina patient without health insurance traveled to Escorts Heart Institute in New Delhi to receive a heart valve replacement operation. The operation would have cost $200,000 in the U.S., but it cost the patient just $10,000, including airfare. Developed-world patients are traveling to the developing world for cosmetic surgery, cardiac care, organ transplants, and eye surgery. A full face-lift that might cost $8,000 to $20,000 in the U.S. costs $2,682 in Thailand. In addition to medical tourism, a rapid influx of immigrants from the developed world are retiring in developing countries such as Mexico and Costa Rica, which have a lower cost of living.

Medical travel to these destinations is growing at more than 20 percent per year. Thailand's Bumrungrad Hospital treated 300,000 foreign patients from 130 nations in 2003, a quarter of its total patients. It fields a help desk that offers assistance in 12 different languages. Foreigners spent about $470 million on health care in Thailand hospitals in 2003. Apollo Hospitals in India, started by Dr. Prathap C. Reddy, has created the largest chain of hospitals outside the U.S. by focusing on the needs of developing nations and international visitors. Apollo offers everything from hospital back-office data processing to surgery in a chain of 35 hospitals with more than 6,000 beds in South Asia. Its website offers fixed prices for procedures in U.S. dollars, such as a $120 executive checkup (including blood work,

EKG, liver function tests, lipid profile, and cardiac stress test) or a breast augmentation for $1,400.

While much of the $40 billion spent annually on global health tourism goes toward more traditional visits by wealthy travelers from developing countries with limited health care to specialists in the U.S., Europe, and other developed markets, the flows of health travel are increasingly moving in the opposite direction.

Other services use digital channels to "transport" customers from the developed world to them. Indian outsourcing firm Wipro, founded by Prem Azimji, has created significant businesses in off-shore services. By linking overseas customers with lower-cost Indian workers, Scott Bayman and Pramod Bhasin built GE Capital International Services to $400 million in revenue before selling a 60 percent stake in the operation to two U.S. private equity firms in November 2004. The sale, for $500 million, was the largest ever involving a business process outsourcing company. Founded in 1981 with a $250 investment by Chairman Narayana Murthy and six part-ners, including current CEO Nandan Nilekani, Infosys became the first Indian company listed on NASDAQ in 1999, with a market cap-italization that grew to more than $11 billion in 2004.

Outsourced customer contact centers in Asia generate $4 billion in annual revenue and are expected to grow by 15 percent per year. Companies are starting to move debt collection overseas. Drug companies such as Novartis, Roche, and Pfizer are turning to China and India for research and development, either at their own facili-ties or through partners to access highly educated but less-expen-sive researchers. These research labs help control costs in an increasingly competitive and price-conscious U.S. market. Product safety testing is also following manufacturing overseas. What other opportunities are there to bring customers physically or virtually into the 86 percent world?

Strategy #8: Utilizing Old Skills in New Ways

Companies can find ways to utilize traditional skills in new ways as the market develops. For example, traditional craftsmen in Bangalore have been retrained as artists in the video and animation industries. Chinese companies such as Global Digital Creations Holdings in Shenzhen are using low-cost advantages and skilled computer workers to begin challenging Pixar and Disney in global animation. While the emerging industry is decidedly high-tech, it draws on a long tradition of Asian film animation in Shanghai that dates back to the 1920s. Led by the Shanghai Animation Film Studio, the industry provided many of the cartoon shows on American television in the 1980s. As emerging markets develop, companies should look for opportunities to draw on countries' historical capabilities while applying these strengths in new ways.

Four Paths

IT companies such as Tata Consultancy Services, Wipro, Infosys, and Satyam in India have found rich opportunities by focusing the resources of the developing world on the needs of the developed world. Some 85 percent of the output of India's software and IT-enabled services is exported, primarily to the developed world. These companies are helping raise their employees' standard of living, in a sector employing 800,000 people in India, and improve their regions. (Although India's IT firms have grabbed headlines, a sense of perspective is needed. The top five IT companies in India combined accounted for only about $5 billion in revenue in 2004, roughly equivalent to the sales of U.S. toy maker Mattel.)

But it is ironic that the world's best customer service is being delivered in developing countries—such as India, Panama, the Philippines, and the Czech Republic—that have a lack of consumerism and service standards. (This lack of a customer culture does sometimes make it more difficult to engage in strategies such as cross-selling and upselling.) Should some of this capacity for excellent service be applied to the local market? Can companies bring this innovation and knowledge to the challenges of their own countries? Are some companies that are focused on the 14 percent markets overlooking the 86 percent opportunity right in front of them?

Firms in the developing and developed world face four paths (A, B, C, and D), as shown in Figure 10-1. Some companies from the 86 percent markets, such as Infosys, focus on serving developed markets (D). Other companies from the developing world, such as two-wheeler maker Hero in India, founded and led by Brijmohan Lall Munjal, and bakery Grupo Bimbo in Mexico are focusing on opportunities close at home or in other 86 percent markets (B). At the same time, many companies from the developed world, from car companies such as General Motors to personal care product manufacturers such as Procter & Gamble, are moving into the developing world to seize the 86 percent opportunities (A). Other firms in developed countries, in the bottom-left corner (C), focus on 14 percent markets, where the field is crowded, growth is slow, and competition is intense.

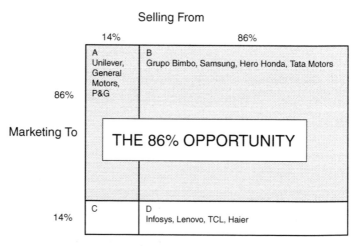

FIGURE 10-1 While the traditional focus has been on the lower-left corner (C), the biggest opportunities for the future are in marketing to the 86 percent world (A and B).

These four strategies also have some public policy implications, because different regulations encourage different approaches. If developing countries have incentives that encourage exporting their goods and services to developed markets, companies tend to overlook opportunities closer to home. Regulations and trade policies need to be designed in a way that balances the pursuit of the 14 percent markets of the developed world with focusing entrepreneurial attention on the needs of markets at home.

Although there is not one path to prosperity and growth, companies need to recognize that the bulk of the world's population is in developing countries. Managers, particularly in developing markets, should look carefully at the opportunities that might be in front of them.

Evolving Opportunities

The paths that companies choose in their own development will affect their future growth and the development of the nations in which they operate. In the next half-century or less, the 86 percent markets will likely face some of the same challenges as the developed world. These nations will have to deal with the many ripple effects of development, such as aging populations.

But on the way to these developed-nation challenges, there will be at least several decades of growth opportunities. China and India won't be developed in the span of most of our careers. In this more-immediate long term, the dynamics of these markets will present tremendous opportunities and demand a rethinking of the market strategies that worked well in the developed world or even in a particular company at an earlier point in time.

With intense competition, a shifting customer base, and emerging technologies, companies cannot afford to stand still. Even if they have a successful formula for today, companies need to keep testing the waters. These ongoing experiments help them learn about the market and reveal the strategies that will work for that particular market at that particular time. Developing markets are full of surprises as they develop. Companies need to be there with customers to understand the next innovations that are needed. A variety of small experiments can help keep the unpleasant surprises small and inexpensive while identifying rich opportunities.

The 86 Percent Solution

- Look for the patterns of change in your markets. Consider how they affect opportunities for specific products or services.

- Study the patterns of evolution of developed markets. How do you expect the trajectory of your current emerging markets to be similar or different?

- Examine opportunities to export successes from one developing market to other emerging markets.

- Explore how you can use a country's past history (even negative history, such as colonization) as a launchpad for expansion.

- Look for opportunities to export developed-market customers such as medical tourists to emerging markets or use technology to virtually transport these customers.

- Find ways to export products that are battle-tested in emerging markets to developed markets.

- As these markets continue to change, look for how you need to change your own offerings and strategies to keep up.

Notes

1 Abraham Maslow. *Motivation and Personality*, Second Edition, Harper & Row, 1970.

CONCLUSION:
AN OPPORTUNITY
NOT TO BE MISSED

As you have seen, the solutions for the 86 percent markets are different from those for the 14 percent world. Developing and implementing these solutions demands creativity and drive to overcome obstacles and adapt to local conditions. To realize the opportunities of the 86 percent markets, companies, NGOs, governments, and other players need to encourage the entrepreneurship required. Developing countries need to take charge and address their own problems rather than looking to the developed world. "Don't ask for jobs; create jobs" should be the slogan in every university and institution to encourage young people to take charge.

This book was sparked by one simple question: Can the 86 percent world stand on its own two feet? The answer is yes. The past 50 years have proven that it can. Entrepreneurs in South Korea, India, China, Mexico, Brazil, South Africa, Egypt, and other countries have shown that they can develop solutions for the 86 percent markets. Driven by microfinancing, entrepreneurs account for nearly seven in 10 adults in developing countries. A survey released in 2005 by Babson College and the London School of Business found that 73 million of the 784 million people surveyed in 34 countries were owners of a new business. Even in Mumbai's Dharavi, one of Asia's largest slums (covering more than 500 acres and accounting for half the city's population), small entrepreneurs produce goods worth more than US$500 million per year. People who have problems will come up with solutions if given the chance.

Companies in developing countries that are now serving 14 percent markets should examine more carefully the opportunities at home. Managers at all companies that currently have little presence in developing markets need to create a coherent strategy for addressing the needs of these markets today and in the future. Companies such as Unilever and Nestlé, Nokia and LG, which had relatively small domestic markets, have been forced to be more aggressive in looking abroad for opportunities. Other companies with large domestic markets now need to try to cultivate a similar sense of urgency. With population shifts, today's large domestic markets will start to shrink, so this urgency may be justified. This shift may take decades, but it also can take years or decades of experience for companies to cultivate the local understanding of developing markets needed to develop coherent solutions. How many companies have well-designed strategies for developing markets? How many companies have the right product designs, brands, and distribution for these markets? How many firms have research centers focused on developing solutions for these markets?

Leaders of companies also need to cultivate awareness of developing markets. PriceWaterhouseCoopers has started a program that sends high-potential, mid-career consultants to developing nations for eight-week pro bono assignments. The "Ulysses Program" tests their talents in extreme conditions and expands their awareness of the realities of developing markets. This type of experience is critical for managers who want to understand the solutions that work in the 86 percent markets.

Nations, NGOs, and universities play a central role in development. Restrictive government policies and unpredictable legislative changes can stifle business growth. Countries that encourage globalization, such as Brazil, China, Hungary, India, and Mexico, increased their GDP per capita by 5 percent in the 1990s, while the less-globalized countries actually saw their GDP per capita decline during this period.[1] Clearly, political and economic policy affect whether countries can tap into the opportunities of global markets. There is also resistance from the developed world, including domestic U.S. opposition to offshoring and national security concerns about the sale of IBM's PC business to Lenovo. Such concerns and opposition are likely to rise as developing markets become increasingly significant in global economics.

There are many opportunities for new initiatives to focus more attention on innovations and leadership for the 86 percent markets. Shouldn't there be recognition for the "best developing-world product designs" in the same way that *BusinessWeek* and *Fortune* highlight "best products" for developed markets in annual issues? Why not create annual awards for the best CEOs in these regions? Shouldn't there be an international conference, similar to the COMDEX convention in information technology, that would give companies an opportunity to showcase the latest innovations that specifically solve the problems of the developing world? Can we create new public-private consortia, similar to the U.S. Sementech initiative in chipmaking, focused on the leapfrog technologies for developing countries? Along with MIT's International Motor Vehicle Program, shouldn't we have a global two-wheeler program to provide similar attention to this important segment of the transportation industry? Shouldn't major technological universities be developing educational programs offering advanced degrees in applying technological solutions for developing economies? Shouldn't we be looking at Africa as a viable market? Can the leading business schools in developed countries create an "86 percent marketing institute" fund research to identify and refine market strategies for developing markets such as the ones discussed in this book? Shouldn't there be new centers for entrepreneurship for these markets?

Why should we do this? It is not just to improve the quality of life in these countries (although this, in itself, is a noble aim). These initiatives are needed to identify the opportunities for future business growth. These solutions improve people's lives, but this is not charity. It is business. These markets are spending trillions of dollars on goods and services, and this spending will only increase as they develop. Companies that want to continue to be major firms in a decade or two have to learn to play successfully in these markets.

A Complex Tapestry

Although this book has focused primarily on the developing world, the interrelationships between people of developing and developed countries will be a big part of the progress of emerging economies and the growth opportunities of developed ones. The world is interlinked in many ways, and these linkages create a complex tapestry. As noted in Chapter 3, "Aim for the Ricochet Economy," social networks span the world, creating "nations" within nations and "nations" across nations. The interactions across these societies sometimes create unexpected relationships. Chinese manufacturer Boto, for example, in a country that is primarily Taoist and Buddhist (and officially atheist), exported more than US$1 billion worth of high-tech artificial Christmas trees in 2004, mostly to the U.S. South Korea, a traditionally Confucian and Buddhist country, is the second-largest source of Christian missionaries in the world. The policies and progress of one country affect others in fundamental ways, from the impact of the rise of China and India on U.S. businesses to the effect of U.S. concerns about homeland security after the 9/11 terrorist attacks on the flow of goods and people (particularly university students and skilled workers) into America. These restrictions mean that the cost of products imported from developing countries will go up and talented students will be shut out.

The shifts in Indian pharmaceuticals indicate the complexities of developing-market ecosystems. Tougher Indian drug patent regulations, legislated by the Indian government in 2005 as a condition for India to join the World Trade Organization, may encourage India's generic drug industry to focus more attention on the U.S. and other developed markets. This has raised critical concerns about the cost of drugs in Africa and other parts of the developing world, where exports from Indian manufacturers such as Cipla and Ranbaxy have helped reduce the cost of antiretroviral AIDS treatments from $15,000 per patient a decade ago to about $200. As India looks to forge closer ties to the 14 percent developed world, who will meet the needs of vulnerable populations in the 86 percent markets?

Rising incomes also mean that countries need to continue to transform themselves. With rising Mexican wages and competition from China and other parts of the world, Mexico lost more than 270,000 manufacturing jobs from 2000 to 2004. As their initial low-cost advantage fades, developing countries will need to navigate the transition to higher value-added activities to sustain their momentum.

Convergence of Civilizations

While Samuel Huntington once presented a view of world civilizations as disconnected islands headed toward a "clash of civilizations" (and there are certainly many opportunities for conflict), there is a countervailing force of connections among different countries, cultures, and economies.[2] These connections are facilitating growth and progress for both developing and developed countries. We cannot limit our thinking with preconceived notions about borders between societies or simple views of gaps between the developed and developing world. Opportunities often emerge across these borders. The developing world can be a source of solutions that are tremendously valuable to the developed world, and vice versa. Even terms such as "developing" and "developed" are an oversimplification of this complex interweaving of cultures and economies that is occurring on a global scale.

The relief efforts after the tsunami that hit Asia in December 2004 highlighted for the world how precarious and volatile the situation is in developing countries. Does it take a tsunami to make us realize this? Should there be a "tsunami initiative" that will focus attention on the ongoing lack of infrastructure, water, and other basic necessities in these areas? The disaster also highlighted the growing will and capacity of developing countries to be self-sufficient, with India turning down foreign aid. In the words of one Western diplomat, India "wants to see itself as part of the solution, not part of the problem."[3]

The characteristics of developing nations present both dangers and opportunities for the planet. For example, the youth bulge that can be an engine for growth, as discussed in Chapter 5, "Think Young," could also be a powder keg for conflict. Young people make up most of the militias of the developing world and can contribute significantly to civil unrest. A 2003 study by Population Action International, for example, found that countries with youth bulges (where young people make up more than 40 percent of adults) were about 2.5 times more likely to experience an outbreak of civil war in the 1990s than other countries.

The negative impact of the youth bulge is not inevitable, however. A study of developing countries from 1950 to 2000 concluded that a combination of youth bulges, poor economic performance, and limited opportunities for migration can lead to explosive situations.[4] Countries with robust economic conditions might transform potentially militant youth populations into more productive consumer markets and workforces. Thus, developing and developed countries need each other. They must urgently work to develop vibrant economic conditions, not just for their quality of life but to increase their political stability.

Rising incomes have a positive impact on quality of life—up to a point. The Worldwatch Institute's World Values Survey of 65 countries between 1990 and 2000 indicated that assessment of life satisfaction increased with rising income up to about US$13,000 annual per capita income in purchasing power parity. (After that, added income contributed only modestly to self-reported happiness.)

Realizing the Gains

There is no guarantee that rising profits in the developing world will lead to true economic progress for citizens. Sound economic and political policy is needed to ensure that this rising economic prosperity lifts all boats. By and large, economic growth in developing countries has led to poverty reduction, meaning that individual citizens are benefiting from the broader economic progress. In particular, countries such as Uganda, India, China, and Vietnam have seen poverty reduction rates that are closely related to growth.

Much work still needs to be done. Although global poverty is being reduced, half the world's workers still make less than $2 per day, and more than 1 billion people make less than $1 per day. In fact, a 2004 United Nations report reached the troubling conclusion that the number of people going hungry around the world increased for the first time in nine years, reaching 852 million. This is at a time when U.S. consumers are facing an "epidemic" of obesity and spending billions of dollars to lose weight. (Ironically, this is becoming an increasing concern in developing countries as they develop. A 2005 report in Brazil, for example, found that while 4 million Brazilians are undernourished, some 10 million adults, or 40 percent of the population, are overweight.) UNICEF reported in 2004 that 1 billion of the world's children are severely threatened by hunger, disease, exploitation, or lack of security. Although a majority of the world's children attend school, more than 130 million primary-school-age children in developing countries do not—of whom more than half live in India, Bangladesh, Pakistan, Nigeria, and Ethiopia.

Developing countries have clothed the world, with Bangladesh exporting $4.5 billion in clothing and textiles in 2002, accounting for 74 percent of its exports. While these exports have clothed customers in the developed world, many of the citizens of these same develop- ing countries lack adequate clothing, food, water, and sanitation themselves. Governments can make a difference in these outcomes. This impact can be seen in the fact that although hunger increased globally, 30 countries in Africa, Asia, and Latin America cut the per- centage of hungry people by 25 percent over the last decade by reducing conflicts and promoting rural development.

Just as economic progress doesn't ensure rising living standards across the board, strong revenue and market growth also don't always guarantee company profits. A survey from the *China Economic Quarterly*, for example, found that while U.S. companies in China built profitable businesses, the profits were not as high as in some smaller, slower-growth markets. While U.S. firms generated $4.4 billion in earnings in China in 2003, they *took home* $14.3 billion in Mexico. Low margins and cutthroat competition, because of local skill and efficiency, were blamed for why many foreign firms are still struggling to make any money in China. Although these markets are growing, it will still take astute understanding of markets and effective business models for individual companies to realize profits from this growth.

NGOs are helping ensure that economic gains translate into a better quality of life for the 86 percent countries. This is particularly true of initiatives led by returning expatriates. They have such a pas- sion to ensure that others can share in their newfound prosperity, education, and development. They have expertise and private-sector experience that offer a professional approach to solving long-standing problems. They want to ensure that no one is left behind. Although there is much to be done, the results of their work are nothing short of phenomenal.

Population Equals Profits

In the long run, numbers are on the side of the developing world. The recent emergence of China and India demonstrates how quickly these large populations can become thriving consumer markets. Two decades ago, who would have expected these two countries to be driving the global economy? Who could have seen that war-torn South Korea would emerge as a thriving global player? Who would have thought that Singapore could have emerged as such a strong economy before former Prime Minister Lee Kwan Yew proved it could be done?

The transformation is just beginning. There will be hiccups along the way and further surprises over the next two decades as the next "Chinas" and "Indias" emerge. The only certainty is that 86 percent markets are here to stay. These markets are young and growing. Even though they won't become developed tomorrow, they are the future. And the companies that can develop the right solutions to meet their needs will find a rich source of growth.

Notes

1 *Globalization, Growth and Poverty.* World Bank and Oxford University Press, 2002, pp. 5–6.

2 Samuel Huntington. *The Clash of Civilizations and the Remaking of World Order.* New York: Simon & Schuster, 1996.

3 Edward Luce. "India Defends Refusal to Accept Foreign Aid." *The Financial Times,* January 5, 2005.

4 "Population and Its Discontents." *WorldWatch Magazine,* WorldWatch Institute, September/October 2004, p. 21; and Henrik Urdal. "The Devil in the Demographics: The Effect of Youth Bulges on Domestic Armed Conflict." *World Bank: Social Development Papers,* Paper #14, July 2004.

INDEX

A

aging versus youthful populations, 97-99

Arabic language, 83

Association for India's Development (AID), 196

automobile market, 14

Avahan AIDS prevention initiative, 195

B

banking, 181
  accounts, opening by immigrants, 59

Bengali language, 83

Berbers of North Africa, festival markets, 179

Bill & Melinda Gates Foundation, 40
  fighting spread of AIDS, 195
  foreign enrollment in U.S. colleges, 107

Bollywood films, 102
  releases in India, 11-12

boreholers (sales reps), 171-172, 175, 179

brand consciousness, 79-80
  global brand names
    addressing liabilities of, 86-88
    advertising in rural areas, 89-90
    lack of global brands in developing countries, 76-77
    meanings of global brand names to developing countries, 86
    stretching without breaking, 88-89
    tailoring to local markets, 81-83
  local brand names, 74
    growth, 85
    use by global brands to gain sales, 84-85

C

cable TV piracy, 137

cameras, battery-powered, 131

carnivals for marketing and distribution opportunities, 180

chaebols (business groups), 137

X-Z

Xiaolingtong, 166

youthful population market in
        developing countries, 95

allegiance to both local and global
        cultures, 103-105

awareness

*of changing roles of women,
        109-110*

of influencers, 105

*of opportunities for education,
        106-108*

focus

on migration into cities, 108

on young parents, 106

*on youthful products/services,
        100-102*

growth of consuming class,
        99-100

MTV programming, 95-97

political and economic power,
        102-103

versus developed countries aging
        population, 97-99

"Great schools have... endeavored to do more than keep up to the respectable standard of a recent past; they have labored to supply the needs of an advancing and exacting world..."

— **Joseph Wharton,** *Entrepreneur and Founder of the Wharton School*

The Wharton School is recognized around the world for its innovative leadership and broad academic strengths across every major discipline and at every level of business education. It is one of four undergraduate and 12 graduate and professional schools of the University of Pennsylvania. Founded in 1881 as the nation's first collegiate business school, Wharton is dedicated to creating the highest value and impact on the practice of business and management worldwide through intellectual leadership and innovation in teaching, research, publishing and service.

Wharton's tradition of innovation includes many firsts—the first business textbooks, the first research center, the MBA in health care management—and continues to innovate with new programs, new learning approaches, and new initiatives. Today Wharton is an interconnected community of students, faculty, and alumni who are shaping global business education, practice, and policy.

Wharton is located in the center of the University of Pennsylvania (Penn) in Philadelphia, the fifth-largest city in the United States. Students and faculty enjoy some of the world's most technologically advanced academic facilities. In the midst of Penn's tree-lined, 269-acre urban campus, Wharton students have access to the full resources of an Ivy League university, including libraries, museums, galleries, athletic facilities, and performance halls. In recent years, Wharton has expanded access to its management education with the addition of Wharton West, a San Francisco academic center, and The Alliance with INSEAD in France, creating a global network.

Wharton
UNIVERSITY *of* PENNSYLVANIA

University of Pennsylvania

www.wharton.upenn.edu

Academic Programs:

Wharton continues to pioneer innovations in education across its leading undergraduate, MBA, executive MBA, doctoral, and executive education programs.

More information about Wharton's academic programs can be found at:
http://www.wharton.upenn.edu/academics

Executive Education:

Wharton Executive Education is committed to offering programs that equip executives with the tools and skills to compete, and meet the challenges inherent in today's corporate environment. With a mix of more than 200 programs, including both open enrollment and custom offerings, a world-class faculty, and educational facilities second to none, Wharton offers leading-edge solutions to close to 10,000 executives annually, worldwide.

For more information and a complete program listing:
execed@wharton.upenn.edu (sub 4033)
215.898.1776 or 800.255.3932 ext. 4033
http://execed.wharton.upenn.edu

Research and Analysis:

Knowledge@Wharton is a unique, free resource that offers the best of business—the latest trends; the latest research on a vast range of business issues; original insights of Wharton faculty; studies, paper and analyses of hundreds of topics and industries. *Knowledge@Wharton* has over 400,000 users from more than 189 countries.

For free subscription:
http://knowledge.wharton.upenn.edu

For licensing and content information, please contact:
Jamie Hammond,
Associate Marketing Director,
hammondj@wharton.upenn.edu • 215.898.2388

Wharton School Publishing:

Wharton School Publishing is an innovative new player in global publishing, dedicated to providing thoughtful business readers access to practical knowledge and actionable ideas that add impact and value to their professional lives. All titles are approved by a Wharton senior faculty review board to ensure they are relevant, timely, important, empirically based and/or conceptually sound, and implementable.

For author inquiries or information about corporate education and affinity programs or, please contact:
Barbara Gydé, Managing Director,
gydeb@wharton.upenn.edu • 215.898.4764

The Wharton School: http://www.wharton.upenn.edu
Executive Education: http://execed.wharton.upenn.edu
Wharton School Publishing: http://whartonsp.com
Knowledge@Wharton: http://knowledge.wharton.upenn.edu

The Fortune at the Bottom of the Pyramid
Eradicating Poverty Through Profits

BY C. K. PRAHALAD

The world's most exciting, fastest-growing new market? It's where you least expect it: at the bottom of the pyramid. Collectively, the world's billions of poor people have immense entrepreneurial capabilities and buying power. You can learn how to serve them and help millions of the world's poorest people escape poverty. It is being done—profitably. Whether you're a business leader or an anti-poverty activist, business guru Prahalad shows why you can't afford to ignore "Bottom of the Pyramid" (BOP) markets.

ISBN 0131467506, © 2005, 432 pp., $28.95

Capitalism at the Crossroads
The Unlimited Business Opportunities in Solving the World's Most Difficult Problems

BY STUART L. HART

Capitalism is indeed at a crossroads, facing international terrorism, worldwide environmental change, and an accelerating backlash against globalization. Your company is at a crossroads, too: finding new strategies for profitable growth is now more challenging than it has ever been. Both sets of problems are intimately linked. In this book you'll learn how to identify sustainable products and technologies that can drive new growth while also helping to solve today's most crucial social and environmental problems. Drawing on his experience consulting with leading companies and NGOs worldwide, Hart shows how to become truly indigenous to all your markets—and avoid the pitfalls of traditional 'greening' and 'sustainability' strategies. This book doesn't just point the way to a capitalism that is more inclusive and more welcome: it offers specific techniques you can use to recharge innovation, growth, and profitability in your enterprise.

ISBN 0131439871, © 2005, 288 pp., $27.95